# COURAGE

## The Joy of Living Dangerously

## osho

·

insights for a
new way of living

St. Martin's Griffin ✖ New York

*Book design by Claire Vaccaro*

Library of Congress Cataloging-in-Publication Data

Osho, 1931–1990.
    Courage : the joy of living dangerously / Osho.
       p.   cm. — (Insights for a new way of living)
    ISBN 0-312-20517-1
    1. Courage—Religious aspects.  I. Title.  II. Series: Osho,
1931–1990. Insights for a new way of living.
BP605.R34C68  1999                99-16439
299'.93—dc21                        CIP

3   5   7   9   10   8   6   4   2

# Contents

# Contents

# Foreword

Don't call it uncertainty—call it wonder.
Don't call it insecurity—call it freedom.

I am not here to give you a dogma—a dogma makes one certain.
I am not here to give you any promise for the future—any
promise for the future makes one secure. I am here simply to
make you alert and aware—that is, to be here now, with all the
insecurity that life is, with all the uncertainty that life is, with all
the danger that life is.

I know you come here seeking some certainty, some creed,
some "ism," somewhere to belong to, someone to rely upon. You
come here out of your fear. You are searching for a sort of beautiful
imprisonment—so that you can live without any awareness.

I would like to make you more insecure, more uncertain—because that's how life is, that's how God is. When there is more insecurity and more danger, the only way to respond to it is by awareness.

There are two possibilities. Either you close your eyes and become dogmatic, become a Christian or a Hindu or a Mohammedan
. . . then you become like an ostrich. It doesn't change life; it simply
closes your eyes. It simply makes you stupid, it simply makes you
unintelligent. In your unintelligence you feel secure—all idiots feel

secure. In fact, only idiots feel secure. A really alive man will always feel insecure. What security can there be?

Life is not a mechanical process; it cannot be certain. It is an unpredictable mystery. Nobody knows what is going to happen the next moment. Not even God that you think resides somewhere in the seventh heaven, not even he—if he is there—not even he knows what is going to happen! . . . because if he knows what is going to happen then life is just bogus, then everything is written beforehand, then everything is destined beforehand. How can he know what is going to happen next, if the future is open? If God knows what is going to happen the next moment, then life is just a dead, mechanical process. Then there is no freedom, and how can life exist without freedom? Then there is no possibility to grow or not to grow. If everything is predestined, then there is no glory, no grandeur. Then you are just robots.

No, nothing is secure. That is my message. Nothing can be secure, because a secure life will be worse than death. Nothing is certain. Life is full of uncertainties, full of surprises—that is its beauty! You can never come to a moment when you can say, "Now I am certain." When you say you are certain, you simply declare your death; you have committed suicide.

Life goes on moving with a thousand and one uncertainties. That's its freedom. Don't call it insecurity.

I can understand why mind calls freedom "insecurity." . . . Have you lived in a jail for a few months or a few years? If you have lived in a jail for a few years, when the day of release comes, the prisoner starts feeling uncertain about the future. Everything was certain in the jail; everything was dead routine. His food was supplied, protection was given to him; there was no fear that he would be hungry next day and there would be no food—nothing like that, everything was certain. Now, suddenly, after many years the jailer comes and says to him, "Now you are going to be released." He starts trembling. Outside the walls of the prison, again there will be uncertainties; again he will have to seek, search; again he will have to live in freedom.

Freedom creates fear. People talk about freedom, but they are afraid. And a man is not yet a man if he is afraid of freedom. I give you freedom; I don't give you security. I give you understanding; I don't give you knowledge. Knowledge will make you certain. If I can give you a formula, a set formula, that there is a God and there is a Holy Ghost and there is an only begotten son, Jesus; there is hell and heaven, and these are the good acts and these are the bad acts; do the sin and you will be in hell, do what I call the virtuous acts and you will be in heaven—finished!—then you are certain. That's why so many people have chosen to be Christians, to be Hindus, to be Mohammedans, to be Jainas—they don't want freedom, they want fixed formulas.

A man was dying—suddenly, in an accident on a road. Nobody knew that he was a Jew, so a priest was called, a Catholic priest. He leaned close to the man—and the man was dying, in the last throes of death—and the priest said, "Do you believe in the Trinity of God the Father, the Holy Ghost, and the son Jesus?"

The man opened his eyes and he said, "Look, here I am dying—and he is talking riddles!"

When death knocks at your door, all your certainties will be simply riddles and foolish. Don't cling to any certainty. Life is uncertain—its very nature is uncertain. And an intelligent man always remains uncertain.

This very readiness to remain in uncertainty is courage. This very readiness to be in uncertainty is trust. An intelligent person is one who remains alert whatsoever the situation—and responds to it with his whole heart. Not that he knows what is going to happen, not that he knows, "Do *this* and *that* will happen." Life is not a science; it is not a cause-and-effect chain. Heat the water to a hundred degrees and it evaporates—it is a certainty. But in real life, nothing is certain like that.

Each individual is a freedom, an unknown freedom. It is impossible to predict, impossible to expect. One has to live in awareness and in understanding.

You come to me seeking knowledge; you want set formulas so that you can cling to them. I don't give you any. In fact, if you have any, I take them away! By and by, I destroy your certainty; by and by, I make you more and more hesitant; by and by, I make you more and more insecure. That is the only thing that has to be done. That's the only thing a Master needs to do!—to leave you in total freedom. In total freedom, with all the possibilities opening, nothing fixed . . . you will have to be aware—nothing else is possible.

This is what I call understanding. If you understand, insecurity is an intrinsic part of life—and good that it is so, because it makes life a freedom, it makes life a continuous surprise. One never knows what is going to happen. It keeps you continuously in wonder. Don't call it uncertainty—call it wonder. Don't call it insecurity— call it freedom.

*You cannot be truthful if you are not courageous*
*You cannot be loving if you are not courageous*
*You cannot be trusting if you are not courageous*
*You cannot inquire into reality if you are not courageous*
*Hence courage comes first*
*   and everything else follows*

# WHAT IS COURAGE?

*In the beginning there is not much difference between the coward and the courageous person. The only difference is, the coward listens to his fears and follows them, and the courageous person puts them aside and goes ahead. The courageous person goes into the unknown in spite of all the fears.*

Courage means going into the unknown in spite of all the fears. Courage does not mean fearlessness. Fearlessness happens if you go on being courageous and more courageous. That is the ultimate experience of courage—fearlessness: That is the fragrance when the courage has become absolute. But in the beginning there is not much difference between the coward and the courageous person. The only difference is that the coward listens to his fears and follows them, and the courageous person puts them aside and goes ahead. The courageous person goes into the unknown in spite of all the fears. He knows the fears, the fears are there.

When you go into the uncharted sea, like Columbus did, there is fear, immense fear, because one never knows what is going to happen. You are leaving the shore of safety. You were perfectly okay, in a way; only one thing was missing—adventure. Going into the unknown gives you a thrill. The heart starts pulsating again;

again you are alive, fully alive. Every fiber of your being is alive because you have accepted the challenge of the unknown.

To accept the challenge of the unknown, in spite of all fears, is courage. The fears are there, but if you go on accepting the challenge again and again, slowly slowly those fears disappear. The experience of the joy that the unknown brings, the great ecstasy that starts happening with the unknown, makes you strong enough, gives you a certain integrity, makes your intelligence sharp. For the first time you start feeling that life is not just a boredom but an adventure. Then slowly slowly fears disappear; then you are always seeking and searching for some adventure.

But basically courage is risking the known for the unknown, the familiar for the unfamiliar, the comfortable for the uncomfortable, arduous pilgrimage to some unknown destination. One never knows whether one will be able to make it or not. It is gambling, but only the gamblers know what life is.

## THE TAO OF COURAGE

Life does not listen to your logic; it goes on its own way, undisturbed. You have to listen to life; life will not listen to your logic, it does not bother about your logic.

When you move into life, what do you see? A great storm comes, and big trees fall. They should survive, according to Charles Darwin, because they are the fittest, strongest, most powerful. Look at an ancient tree, three hundred feet high, three thousand years old. The very presence of the tree creates strength, gives a feeling of strength and power. Millions of roots have spread inside the earth, gone deep, and the tree is standing with power. Of course the tree fights—it doesn't want to yield, to surrender—but after the storm, it has fallen, it is dead, it is no longer alive, and all that strength has gone. The storm was too much—the storm is always too much, because the storm comes from the whole, and a tree is just an individual.

Then there are small plants and ordinary grass—when the storm comes the grass yields, and the storm cannot do any harm to it. At the most it can give it a good cleansing, that's all; all the dirt that has gathered on it is washed away. The storm gives it a good bath, and when the storm has gone, the small plants and the grasses are again dancing high. The grass has almost no roots, it can be pulled out by a small child, but the storm was defeated. What happened?

The grass followed the way of Tao, the way of Lao Tzu, and the big tree followed Charles Darwin. The big tree was very logical: it tried to resist, it tried to show its strength. If you try to show your strength, you will be defeated. All Hitlers, all Napoleons, all Alexanders are big trees, strong trees. They will all be defeated. Lao Tzus are just like small plants: nobody can defeat them because they are always ready to yield. How can you defeat a person who yields, who says, "I am already defeated," who says, "Sir, you enjoy your victory, there is no need to create any trouble. I'm defeated." Even an Alexander will feel futile before a Lao Tzu, he cannot do anything. It happened; it happened exactly like that. . . .

A sannyasin, a mystic by the name of Dandamis, existed in the days of Alexander, in the days when Alexander was in India. Friends had told Alexander when he was leaving for India that when he came back he should bring a sannyasin, because that rare flower flowered only in India. They said, "We would like to see the phenomenon of sannyas, what it is, what exactly a sannyasin is."

He was so engaged in war and struggle and fight that he almost forgot about it, but when he was going back, just on the boundary of India, he suddenly remembered. He was leaving the last village, so he asked his soldiers to go into the village and inquire if there was a sannyasin around there somewhere. By accident Dandamis was there in the village, by the riverside, and the people said, "You have come at the right time. There are many sannyasins, but a *real* sannyasin is always rare, and he is here now. You can have darshan, you can go and visit him."

Alexander laughed. He said, "I'm not here to have darshan, my soldiers will go and fetch him. I will take him back to the capital of my country."

The villagers said, "It won't be so easy. . . ."

Alexander could not believe it—what difficulty could there be? He had conquered emperors, great kings, so with a beggar, a sannyasin, what difficulty could there be? His soldiers went to see this Dandamis, who was standing naked on the bank of the river. They said, "Alexander the Great invites you to accompany him to his country. All comforts, whatsoever you need, will be provided. You will be a royal guest."

The naked fakir laughed and said, "You go and tell your master that a man who calls himself great cannot be great. And nobody can take me anywhere—a sannyasin moves like a cloud, in total freedom. I am not enslaved to anybody."

They said, "You must have heard about Alexander, he is a dangerous man. If you say no to him, he won't listen, he will simply cut your head off!"

Alexander had to go, because the soldiers said, "He is a rare man, luminous, there is something of the unknown around him. He is naked, but you don't feel in his presence that he is naked— later on you remember. He is so powerful that in his presence you simply forget the whole world. He is magnetic, and a great silence surrounds him and the whole area feels as if it is delighting in the man. He is worth seeing, but there seems to be trouble ahead for him, the poor man, because he says that nobody can take him any- where, that he is nobody's slave."

Alexander went to see him with a naked sword in his hand. Dandamis laughed and said, "Put down your sword, it is useless here. Put it back in the sheath; it is useless here because you can cut only my body, and that I left long ago. Your sword cannot cut *me,* so put it back; don't be childish."

And it is said that this was the first time Alexander followed somebody else's order; just because of the very presence of the man, he couldn't remember who he was. He put his sword back in the sheath and said, "I have never come across such a beautiful man." And when he was back in his camp he said, "It is difficult to kill a man who is ready to die, it is meaningless to kill him. You can kill a person who fights, then there is some meaning in killing; but you can't kill a man who is ready and who is saying, 'This is my head, you can cut it off.' "

And Dandamis actually said, "This is my head, you can cut it off. When the head falls, you will see it falling on the sand and I will also see it falling on the sand, because I am not my body. I am a witness."

Alexander had to report to his friends, "There were sannyasins that I could have brought, but they were not sannyasins. Then I came across a man who was really something rare—and you have heard rightly, this flower *is* rare, but nobody can force him because he is not afraid of death. When a person is not afraid of death, how can you force him to do anything?"

It is your fear that makes you a slave—it is your fear. When you are fearless you are no longer a slave; in fact, it is your fear that forces you to make others slaves before they can try to make a slave out of you.

A man who is fearless is neither afraid of anybody nor makes anybody afraid of him. Fear totally disappears.

## THE WAY OF THE HEART

The word *courage* is very interesting. It comes from a Latin root *cor*, which means "heart." So to be courageous means to live with the heart. And weaklings, only weaklings, live with the head; afraid, they create a security of logic around themselves. Fearful, they close every window and door—with theology, concepts, words, theories—and inside those closed doors and windows, they hide.

The way of the heart is the way of courage. It is to live in insecurity; it is to live in love, and trust; it is to move in the unknown. It is leaving the past and allowing the future to be. Courage is to move on dangerous paths. Life is dangerous, and only cowards can avoid the danger—but then, they are already dead. A person who is alive, really alive, vitally alive, will always move into the unknown. There is danger there, but he will take the risk. The heart is always ready to the the risk, the heart is a gambler. The head is a businessman. The head always calculates—it is cunning. The heart is noncalculating.

This English word *courage* is beautiful, very interesting. To live through the heart is to discover meaning. A poet lives through the heart and, by and by, in the heart he starts listening to the sounds of the unknown. The head cannot listen; it is very far away from the unknown. The head is filled with the known.

What is your mind? It is all that you have known. It is the past, the dead, that which has gone. Mind is nothing but the accumulated past, the memory. Heart is the future; heart is always the hope, heart is always somewhere in the future. Head thinks about the past; heart dreams about the future.

The future is yet to come. The future is yet to be. The future has yet a possibility—it will come, it is already coming. Every moment the future is becoming the present, and the present is becoming the past. The past has no possibility, it has been used. You have already moved away from it—it is exhausted, it is a dead thing, it is like a grave. The future is like a seed; it is coming, ever coming, always reaching and meeting with the present. You are always moving. The present is nothing but a movement into the future. It is the step that you have already taken; it is going into the future.

> The heart is always ready to take the risk, the heart is a gambler. The head is a businessman. The head always calculates—it is cunning.

7

EVERYBODY IN THE WORLD WANTS TO BE TRUE because just to be true brings so much joy and such an abundance of blissfulness—why should one be false? You have to have the courage for a little deeper insight: Why are you afraid? What can the world do to you? People can laugh at you, it will do them good—laughter is always a medicine, healthful. People can think you are mad . . . just because they think you are mad, you don't become mad.

> Why are you afraid? What can the world do to you? People can laugh at you, it will do them good—laughter is always a medicine, healthful.

And if you are authentic about your joy, your tears, your dance, sooner or later there will be people who will start understanding you, who may start joining your caravan. I myself had started alone on the path, and then people went on coming and it became a worldwide caravan! And I have not invited anybody; I have simply done whatever I felt was coming from my heart.

My responsibility is toward my heart, not toward anybody else in the world. So is your responsibility only toward your own being. Don't go against it, because going against it is committing suicide, is destroying yourself. And what is the gain? Even if people give you respect, and people think that you are a very sober, respectable, honorable man, these things are not going to nourish your being. They are not going to give you any more insight into life and its tremendous beauty.

How many millions of people have lived before you on this earth? You don't even know their names; whether they ever lived or not does not make any difference. There have been saints and there have been sinners, and there have been very respectable people, and there have been all kinds of eccentrics, crazy, but they have all disappeared—not even a trace has remained on the earth.

Your sole concern should be to take care of and protect those qualities that you can take with you when death destroys your body, your mind, because these qualities will be your sole companions. They are the only real values, and the people who attain them— only they live; others only pretend to live.

The KGB knocks on Yussel Finkelstein's door one dark night. Yussel opens the door. The KGB man barks out, "Does Yussel Finkelstein live here?"

"No," replies Yussel, standing there in his frayed pajamas.

"No? So what is your name then?"

"Yussel Finkelstein."

The KGB man knocks him to the ground and says,

"Did you just say that you did not live here?"

Yussel replies, "You call this living?"

Just living is not always living. Look at your life. Can you call it a blessing? Can you call it a gift, a present of existence? Would you like this life to be given to you again and again?

DON'T LISTEN TO THE SCRIPTURES—listen to your own heart. That is the only scripture I prescribe: listen very attentively, very consciously, and you will never be wrong. And listening to your own heart, you will never be divided. Listening to your own heart, you will start moving in the right direction, without ever thinking of what is right and what is wrong.

The whole art for the new humanity will consist in the secret of listening to the heart consciously, alertly, attentively. And follow it, go wherever it takes you. Yes, sometimes it will take you into dangers—but remember, those dangers are needed to make you ripe. Sometimes it will take you astray—but remember again, those goings astray are part of growth. Many times you will fall—rise up again, because this is how one gathers strength, by falling and rising again. This is how one becomes integrated.

But don't follow rules imposed from the outside. No imposed rule can ever be right—because rules are invented by people who want to rule you! Yes, sometimes there have been great enlightened people in the world, too—a Buddha, a Jesus, a Krishna, a Moham-med. They have not given rules to the world—they have given their love. But sooner or later the disciples gather together and start making codes of conduct. Once the Master is gone, once the light is gone and they are in deep darkness, they start groping for certain rules to follow, because now the light in which they could have seen is no longer there. Now they will have to depend on rules.

What Jesus did was his own heart's whispering, and what Christians go on doing is not their own hearts' whispering. They are imitators—and the moment you imitate you insult your humanity, you insult your God.

Never be an imitator, be always original. Don't become a carbon copy. But that's what is happening all over the world—carbon copies and carbon copies.

Life is really a dance if you are an original—and you are meant to be an original. Just look how different Krishna is from Buddha. If Krishna had followed Buddha, we would have missed one of the most beautiful men of this earth. Or if Buddha had followed Krishna, he would have been just a poor specimen. Just think of Buddha playing on the flute!—he would have disturbed many people's sleep, he was not a flute player. Just think of Buddha dancing; it looks so ridiculous, just absurd.

And the same is the case with Krishna. Sitting underneath a tree with no flute, with no crown of peacock feathers, with no beautiful clothes—just sitting like a beggar under a tree with closed eyes, nobody dancing around him, nothing of the dance, nothing of the song—and Krishna would look so poor, so impoverished. A Buddha is a Buddha, a Krishna is a Krishna, and you are you. And you are not in any way less than anybody else. Respect yourself, respect your own inner voice and follow it.

> A Buddha is a Buddha, a Krishna is a Krishna, and you are you. And you are not in any way less than anybody else. Respect yourself, respect your own inner voice and follow it.

And remember, I am not guaranteeing you that it will always lead you to the right. Many times it will take you to the wrong, because to come to the right door one has to knock first on many wrong doors. That's how it is. If you suddenly stumble upon the right door, you will not be able to recognize that it is right. So remember, in the ultimate reckoning no effort is ever wasted; all efforts contribute to the ultimate climax of your growth.

So don't be hesitant, don't be worried too much about going wrong. That is one of the problems: people have been taught never to do anything wrong, and then they become so hesitant, so fearful, so frightened of doing wrong, that they become stuck. They cannot move, something wrong may happen. So they become like rocks, they lose all movement.

> Commit as many mistakes as possible, remembering only one thing: don't commit the same mistake again.
> And you will be growing.

Commit as many mistakes as possible, remembering only one thing: don't commit the same mistake again. And you will be growing. It is part of your freedom to go astray, it is part of your dignity to go even against God. And it is sometimes beautiful to go even against God. This is how you will start having a spine; otherwise there are millions of people, spineless.

Forget all about what you have been told, "This is right and this is wrong." Life is not so fixed. The thing that is right today may be wrong tomorrow, the thing that is wrong this moment may be right the next moment. Life cannot be pigeonholed; you cannot label it so easily, "This is right and this is wrong." Life is not a chemist's shop where every bottle is labeled and you know what is what. Life is a mystery: one moment something fits and then it is right; another moment, so much water has gone down the Ganges that it no longer fits and it is wrong.

What is my definition of right? That which is harmonious with existence is right, and that which is disharmonious with existence is wrong. You will have to be very alert each moment, because it has to be decided each moment afresh. You cannot depend on ready-made answers for what is right and what is wrong. Only stupid people depend on ready-made answers because then they need not be intelligent, there is no need. You already know what is right and what is wrong, you can memorize the list; the list is not very big.

The Ten Commandments—so simple!—you know what is right and what is wrong. But life goes on changing continuously. If Moses comes back, I don't think he will give you the same ten commandments—he cannot. After three thousand years, how can he give you the same commandments? He will have to invent something new.

But my own understanding is this: whenever commandments are given, they create difficulties for people because by the time they are given they are already out of date. Life moves so fast; it is a dynamism, it is not static. It is not a stagnant pool, it is a Ganges, it goes on flowing. It is never the same for two consecutive moments. So one thing may be right this moment and may not be right the next.

Then what to do? The only possible thing is to make people so aware that they themselves can decide how to respond to a changing life.

A Zen story:

There were two temples, rivals. Both the masters—they must have been only so-called masters, must have really been priests—were so much against each other that they told their followers never to look at the other temple.

*13*

Each of the priests had a boy to serve him, to go and fetch things for him, to go on errands. The priest of the first temple told his boy servant, "Never talk to the other boy. Those people are dangerous."

But boys are boys. One day they met on the road, and the boy from the first temple asked the other, "Where are you going?"

The other said, "Wherever the wind takes me." He must have been listening to great Zen things in the temple; he said, "Wherever the wind takes me." A great statement, pure Tao.

But the first boy was very much embarrassed, offended, and he could not find how to answer him. Frustrated, angry, and also feeling guilty . . . "My master said not to talk with these people. These people really *are* dangerous. Now, what kind of answer is this? He has humiliated me."

He went to his master and told him what had happened: "I am sorry that I talked to him. You were right, those people are strange. What kind of answer is this? I asked him, 'Where are you going?'—a simple, formal question—and I knew he was going to the market, just as I was going to the market. But he said, 'Wherever the wind takes me.' "

> ❧
>
> Whenever commandments are given, they create difficulties for people because by the time they are given they are already out of date. Life moves so fast; it is a dynamism, it is not static.

The master said, "I warned you, but you didn't listen. Now look, tomorrow you stand at the same place again. When he comes, ask him, 'Where are you going?' and he will say, 'Wherever the wind takes me.' Then you also be a little more philosophical. Say, 'If you don't have any legs, then?'—because the soul is bodiless and the wind cannot take the soul anywhere—'What about that?' "

The boy wanted to be absolutely ready; the whole night he repeated it again and again and again. And next morning very early he went there, stood on the right spot, and at the exact time the other boy came. He was very happy, now he was going to show him what real philosophy is. So he asked, "Where are you going?" And he was waiting. . . .

But the boy said, "I am going to fetch vegetables from the market."

Now, what to do with the philosophy he had learned?

Life is like that. You cannot prepare for it, you cannot be ready for it. That's its beauty, that's its wonder, that it always takes you unawares, it always comes as a surprise. If you have eyes you will see that each moment is a surprise and no ready-made answer is ever applicable.

## THE WAY OF INTELLIGENCE

Intelligence is aliveness, it is spontaneity. It is openness, it is vulnerability. It is impartiality, it is the courage to function without conclusions. And why do I say it is a courage? It is a courage because when you function out of a conclusion the conclusion protects you;

the conclusion gives you security, safety. You know it well, you know how to come to it, you are very efficient with it. To function without a conclusion is to function in innocence. There is no security; you may go wrong, you may go astray.

One who is ready to go on the exploration called truth has to be ready also to commit many errors, mistakes—has to be able to risk. One may go astray, but that is how one arrives. Going many many times astray, one learns how not to go astray. Committing many mistakes, one learns what is a mistake and how not to commit it. Knowing what is error, one comes closer and closer to what is truth. It is an individual exploration; you cannot depend on others' conclusions.

> Committing many mistakes, one learns what is a mistake and how not to commit it. Knowing what is error, one comes closer and closer to what is truth. It is an individual exploration; you cannot depend on others' conclusions.

YOU WERE BORN AS A NO-MIND. Let this sink into your heart as deeply as possible because through that, a door opens. If you were born as a no-mind, then the mind is just a social product. It is nothing natural, it is cultivated. It has been put together on top of you. Deep down you are still free, you can get out of it. One can never get out of nature, but one can get out of the artificial any moment one decides to.

Existence precedes thinking. So existence is not a state of mind,

16

it is a state beyond. To *be*, not to think, is the way to know the fundamental. Science means thinking, philosophy means thinking, theology means thinking. Religiousness does not mean thinking. The religious approach is a nonthinking approach. It is more intimate, it brings you closer to reality. It drops all that hinders, it unblocks you; you start flowing into life. You don't think that you are separate, looking. You don't think that you are a watcher, aloof, distant. You meet, mingle, and merge into reality.

And there is a different kind of knowing. It cannot be called "knowledge." It is more like love, less like knowledge. It is so intimate that the word *knowledge* is not sufficient to express it. The word *love* is more adequate, more expressive.

In the history of human consciousness, the first thing that evolved was magic. Magic was a combination of science and religion. Magic had something of the mind and something of the no-mind. Then out of magic grew philosophy. Then out of philosophy grew science. Magic was both no-mind and mind. Philosophy was only mind. And then mind plus experimentation became science. Religiousness is a state of no-mind.

Religiousness and science are the two approaches to reality. Science approaches through the secondary; religiousness goes direct. Science is an indirect approach; religiousness is an immediate approach. Science goes round and round; religiousness simply penetrates to the heart of reality.

A few more things. . . . Thinking can think only about the known—it can chew the already chewed. Thinking can never be original. How can you think about the unknown? Whatsoever you *can* manage to think will belong to the known. You can think only because you know. At the most, thinking can create new combinations. You can think about a horse who flies in the sky, who is made of gold, but nothing is new. You know birds who fly in the sky, you know gold, you know horses; you combine the three together. At the most, thinking can imagine new combinations, but it cannot know the unknown. The unknown remains beyond it. So thinking goes in a circle, goes on knowing the known again and again and again. It goes on chewing the chewed. Thinking is never original.

To come upon reality originally, radically, to come upon reality without any mediator—to come upon reality as if you are the first person to exist—that is liberating. That very newness of it liberates.

TRUTH IS AN EXPERIENCE, NOT A BELIEF. Truth never comes by studying about it; truth has to be encountered, truth has to be faced. The person who studies about love is like the person who studies about the Himalayas by looking at the map of the mountains. The map is not the mountain! And if you start believing in the map, you will go on missing the mountain. If you become too much obsessed with the map, the mountain may be there just in front of you, but still you will not be able to see it.

And that's how it is. The mountain is in front of you, but your eyes are full of maps—maps of the mountain, maps about the same mountain, made by different explorers. Somebody has climbed the mountain from the north side, somebody from the east. They have made different maps: Koran, Bible, Gita—different maps of the same truth. But you are too full of the maps, too burdened by their weight; you cannot move even an inch. You cannot see the mountain just standing in front of you, its virgin snow peaks shining like gold in the morning sun. You don't have the eyes to see it.

The prejudiced eye is blind, the heart full of conclusions is dead. Too many a priori assumptions and your intelligence starts losing its sharpness, its beauty, its intensity. It becomes dull.

Dull intelligence is what is called intellect. Your so-called intelligentsia are not really intelligent, they are just intellectual. Intellect is a corpse. You can decorate it—you can decorate it with great pearls, diamonds, emeralds, but still a corpse is a corpse.

To be alive is a totally different matter.

SCIENCE MEANS BEING DEFINITE, being absolutely definite, about facts. And if you are very definite about facts, then you cannot feel the mysterious—the more definite you are, the more mystery evaporates. Mystery needs a certain vagueness; mystery needs something undefined, undemarcated. Science is factual; mystery is not factual, it is existential.

> The prejudiced eye is blind, the heart full of conclusions is dead. Too many a priori assumptions and your intelligence starts losing its sharpness, its beauty, its intensity. It becomes dull. Dull intelligence is what is called intellect.

A fact is only a part of existence, a very small part, and science deals with parts because it is easier to deal with parts. They are smaller, you can analyze them; you are not overwhelmed by them, you can possess them in your hands. You can dissect them, you can label them, you can be absolutely certain about their qualities, quantities, possibilities—but in that very process mystery is being killed. Science is the murder of mystery.

If you want to experience the mysterious, you will have to enter through another door, from a totally different dimension. The dimension of the mind is the dimension of science, and the dimension of meditation is the dimension of the miraculous, the mysterious.

> Science is the murder of mystery.
> If you want to experience the mysterious, you will have to enter through another door, from a totally different dimension.

Meditation makes everything undefined. Meditation takes you into the unknown, the uncharted. Meditation takes you slowly, slowly into a kind of dissolution where the observer and the observed become one. Now, that is not possible in science. The observer has to be the observer, and the observed has to be the observed, and a clear-cut distinction has to be maintained continuously. Not even for a single moment should you forget yourself; not even for a single moment should you become interested, dissolved, overwhelmed, passionate, loving toward the object of your inquiry. You have to be detached, you have to be very cold—cold, absolutely indifferent. And indifference kills mystery.

If you really want the experience of the mysterious, then you will have to open a new door in your being. I am not saying stop being a scientist; I am simply saying that science can remain a peripheral activity to you. When in the lab be a scientist, but when you come out of the lab forget all about science. Then listen to the birds—and not in a scientific way! Look at the flowers—and not in a scientific way, because when you look at a rose in a scientific way, it is a totally different kind of thing that you are looking at. It is not the same rose that a poet experiences.

The experience does not depend on the object. The experience depends on the experiencer, on the quality of experiencing.

LOOKING AT A FLOWER, BECOME THE FLOWER, dance around the flower, sing a song. The wind is cool and crisp, the sun is warm, and the flower is in its prime. The flower is dancing in the wind, rejoicing, singing a song, singing alleluia. Participate with it! Drop indifference, objectivity, detachment. Drop all your scientific attitudes. Become a little more fluid, more melting, more merging. Let the flower speak to your heart, let the flower enter your being. Invite him—he is a guest! And then you will have some taste of mystery.

This is the first step toward the mysterious, and if you can be a participant for a moment, you have known the key, the secret of the ultimate step. Then become a participant in everything that you are doing. Walking, don't just do it mechanically, don't just go on watching it—be it. Dancing, don't do it technically; technique is irrelevant. You may be technically correct and yet you will miss the whole joy of it. Dissolve yourself in the dance, become the dance, forget about the dancer.

When such deep unity starts happening in many, many phases of your life, when all around you start having such tremendous experiences of disappearance, egolessness, nothingness . . . when the flower is there and you are not, the rainbow is there and you are not . . . when the clouds are roaming in the sky both within and without, and you are not . . . when there is utter silence as far as you are concerned—when there is nobody in you, just a pure silence, a virgin silence, undistracted, undisturbed by logic, thought, emotion, feeling—that is the moment of meditation. Mind is gone, and when mind is gone mystery enters.

> Why don't people trust? Because they don't trust their intelligence. They are afraid, they are afraid that they may be cheated.

## THE WAY OF TRUST

TRUST IS THE GREATEST INTELLIGENCE. Why don't people trust? Because they don't trust their intelligence. They are afraid, they are afraid that they may be cheated. They are afraid; that's why they doubt. Doubt is out of fear. Doubt is out of a kind of insecurity in your own intelligence. You are not so confident that you can trust and you can go into trust. Trust needs great intelligence, courage, integrity. It needs a great heart to go into it. If you don't have enough intelligence, you protect yourself through doubt.

If you have intelligence, you are ready to go into the unknown because you know that even if the whole known world disappears and you are left in the unknown, you will be able to settle there. You will be able to make a home there in the unknown. You trust your intelligence. Doubt is on guard; intelligence keeps itself open because intelligence knows, "Whatsoever happens, I will be able to take the challenge, to respond adequately." The mediocre mind has not that trust in itself. Knowledge is mediocre.

To be in the state of not knowing is intelligence, it is awareness—and it is noncumulative. Each moment that which happens disappears; it leaves no trace behind, no existential trace. One comes out of it again pure, again innocent, again like a child.

Don't try to understand life. Live it! Don't try to understand love. Move into love. Then you will know—and that knowing will come out of your experiencing. That knowing will never destroy the mystery: the more you know, the more you know that much remains to be known.

Life is not a problem. To look at it as a problem is to take a wrong step. It is a mystery to be lived, loved, experienced.

In fact, the mind that is always after explanations is an afraid mind. Because of great fear he wants everything to be explained. He cannot go into anything before it is explained to him. With explanations he feels that now the territory is familiar; now he knows the geography, now he can move with the map and the guidebook and the timetable. He is never ready to move in an unknown territory, uncharted, without a map, without a guide. But life is like that, and no map is possible because life goes on changing. Every moment it is now. There is nothing old under the sun, I say to you: everything

> Life is not a problem. To look at it as a problem is to take a wrong step. It is a mystery to be lived, loved, experienced.

is new. It is a tremendous dynamism, an absolute movement. Only change is permanent, only change never changes.

Everything else goes on changing, so you cannot have a map; by the time the map is ready it is already out of date. By the time the map is available it is useless, life has changed its tracks. Life has started playing a new game. You cannot cope with life with maps because it is not measurable, and you cannot cope with life by consulting guidebooks because guidebooks are possible only if things are stagnant. Life is not stagnant—it is a dynamism, it is a process. You cannot have a map of it. It is not measurable, it is an unmeasurable mystery. Don't ask for explanations.

And this I call maturity of mind: when somebody comes to the point of looking at life without any questions, and simply dives into it with courage and fearlessness.

THE WHOLE WORLD IS FULL OF PSEUDORELIGIOUS PEOPLE—churches, temples, *gurudwaras*, mosques, full of religious people. And can't you see that the world is absolutely irreligious? With so many religious people, the world is so irreligious—how is this miracle happening? Everybody is religious and the total is ir-religiousness. The religion is false. People have "cultivated" trust. Trust has become a belief, not an experience. They have been taught to believe, they have not been taught to know—that's where humanity has missed.

Never believe. If you cannot trust it is better to doubt, because through doubt, someday or other the possibility of trust will arise. You cannot live with doubt eternally. Doubt is disease; it is an illness. In doubt you can never feel fulfilled; in doubt you will always tremble; in doubt you will always remain in anguish and divided and indecisive. In doubt you will remain in a nightmare. So one day or other you will start seeking how to go beyond it. So I say it is good to be an atheist rather than a theist, a pseudotheist.

You have been taught to believe—from the very childhood, everybody's mind has been conditioned to believe: believe in God, believe in the soul, believe in this and believe in that. Now that belief has entered into your bones and your blood, but it remains a belief—you have not known. And unless you *know*, you cannot be liberated. Knowledge liberates, only knowing liberates. All beliefs are borrowed; others have given them to you, they are not your flowerings. And how can a borrowed thing lead you toward the real, the absolutely real? Drop all that you have taken from others. It is better to be a beggar than to be rich—rich not by your own earning but rich through stolen goods; rich through borrowed things, rich through tradition, rich through heritage. No, it is better to be a beggar but to be on one's own. That poverty has a richness in it because it is true, and your richness of belief is very poor. Those beliefs can never go very deep; they remain skin-deep at the most. Scratch a little, and the disbelief comes out.

> This I call maturity of mind: when somebody comes to the point of looking at life without any questions, and simply dives into it with courage and fearlessness.

You believe in God; then your business fails and suddenly the disbelief is there. You say, "I don't believe, I cannot believe in God." You believe in God and your beloved dies, and the disbelief comes up. You believe in God and just by the death of your beloved the belief is destroyed? It is not worth much. Trust can never be destroyed—once it is there, nothing can destroy it. Nothing, absolutely nothing can destroy it.

> ≈
>
> All beliefs are borrowed, others have given them to you, they are not your flowerings. And how can a borrowed thing lead you toward the real?

So remember, there is a great difference between trust and belief. Trust is personal; belief is social. Trust you have to grow in; belief you can remain in, whatsoever you are, and belief can be imposed on you. Drop beliefs. The fear will be there— because if you drop belief, doubt arises. Each belief is forcing doubt into hiding somewhere, repressing doubt. Don't be worried about it; let the doubt come. Everybody has to pass through a dark night before he reaches the sunrise. Everybody has to pass through doubt. Long is the journey, dark is the night. But when after the long journey and the dark night the morning arises, then you know it was all worthwhile. Trust cannot be "cultivated"—and never try to cultivate it; that is what has been done by the whole of humanity. Cultivated trust becomes belief. Discover trust within yourself, don't cultivate it. Go deeper into your being, to the very source of your being, and discover it.

INQUIRY WILL NEED TRUST because you will be going into the unknown. It will demand tremendous trust and courage because you are moving away from the conventional and the traditional; you are moving away from the crowd. You are going into the open sea and you don't know whether the other shore exists at all.

I could not send you into such an inquiry without preparing you to have trust. It will look contradictory, but what can I do?—this is how life is. Only a man of great trust is capable of great doubt, great inquiry.

A man of little trust can only doubt a little. A man of no trust can only pretend that he doubts. He cannot inquire deeply. The depth comes through trust—and it is a risk. Before I send you into the uncharted sea, I have to prepare you for this immense journey on which you will have to go alone—but I can lead you up to the boat. First you have to know about the beauty of trust, the ecstasy

> ➣
>
> Trust is personal, belief is social. Trust you have to grow in, belief you can remain in, whatsoever you are, and belief can be imposed on you. Drop beliefs.

of the way of the heart—so when you go into the open ocean of reality you will have courage enough to keep on going. Whatever happens you will have trust enough in yourself

Just see it: how can you trust anybody or anything if you don't trust yourself? It is impossible. If you doubt yourself how can you trust? It is you who are going to trust, and you don't trust yourself—how can you trust your trust? It is absolutely necessary that the heart should be opened before intellect can be transformed into intelligence. That's the difference between intellect and intelligence.

Intelligence is intellect in tune with your heart.

The heart knows how to trust.

The intellect knows how to seek and search.

There is an old Eastern story:

Two beggars used to live outside a village. One was blind and one had no legs. One day the forest near the village, where these beggars used to live, caught fire. They were competitors, of course—in the same profession, begging from the same people—and they were continually angry with each other. They were enemies, not friends.

> A man of little trust
> can only doubt a
> little.
> A man of no trust
> can only pretend that
> he doubts.
> He cannot inquire
> deeply. The depth
> comes through trust—
> and it is a risk.

People in the same profession cannot be friends. It is very difficult because it is a question of competition, clients—you take away somebody's client. Beggars label their clients: "Remember that this is my man; don't you bother him." You don't know to which beggar you belong, who the beggar is whose possession you are, but some beggar on the street has possessed you. He may have fought and won the battle and now you are his possession. . . .

I used to see a beggar near the university; one day I found him in the market. He was constantly there, near the university, because young people are more generous; older people slowly become more miserly, more afraid. Death is coming close by, now money seems to be the only thing that can help. And if they have money then others may help them also; if they don't have money even their own sons, their own daughters, won't bother about them. But young people can be spendthrifts. They are young, they can earn; life is there, a long life ahead.

He was a rich beggar because in India a student reaches university only if he comes from a rich family; otherwise it is a struggle. A few poor people also get there, but it is painful, arduous. I was also from a poor family. The whole night I was working as an editor of a newspaper, and in the day I went to the university. For years I could not sleep more than three or four hours—whenever I could find time in the day or in the night.

So this beggar was very strong. No other beggar could enter the university street, even entry was banned. Everybody knew to whom the university belonged—to that beggar! One day suddenly I saw a young man; the old man was not there. I asked him, "What happened? Where is the old man?"

He said, "He is my father-in-law. He has given the university to me as a gift." Now, the university did not know that the ownership had changed, that somebody else was now the owner. The young man said, "I have married his girl."

In India a dowry is given when you marry somebody's daughter. It is not just that you marry the daughter: your father-in-law has to give you, if he is very rich, a car, a bungalow. If he is not very rich then at least a scooter; if not that, then at least a bicycle, but he has to give something or other—a radio, a transistor set, a television—and some cash. If he is really rich then he gives you an opportunity to go abroad, to study, to become a more educated person, a doctor, an engineer—and he will pay for it.

This beggar's daughter had got married and as her dowry the young man had been given the whole university. He said, "From today this street and this university belong to me. And my father-in-law has shown me who my clients are."

I saw the old man in the marketplace so I said to him, "Great! You have done well in giving a dowry."

"Yes," he said, "I had only one daughter and I wanted to do something for my son-in-law. I have given him the best place to beg. Now I am here trying again to arrange my monopoly in the market. It is a very tough job here because there are so many beggars, senior ones who have already taken possession of clients. But there is nothing to be worried about. I will manage; I will throw out a few beggars from here"—and certainly he did.

So when the forest was on fire those two beggars thought for a moment. They were enemies, not even on speaking terms, but this was an emergency. The blind man said to the man who had no legs, "Now the only way to escape is that you sit on my shoulders; use my legs and I will use your eyes. That's the only way we can save ourselves."

It was immediately understood. There was no problem. The man without legs could not get out; it was impossible for him to cross the forest—it was all on fire. He could have moved a little bit but that would not help. An exit, and a very quick exit, was needed. The blind man also was certain that he could not get out. He did not know where the fire was, where the road was, and where the trees were burning and where they were not. A blind man . . . he would get lost. But both were intelligent people; they dropped their enmity, became friends, and saved their lives.

This is an Eastern fable. And this is about your intellect and your heart. It has nothing to do with beggars, it has something to do with you. It has nothing to do with the forest on fire, it has something to do with you—because you are on fire. Each moment you are burning, suffering, in misery, anguish. Alone your intellect is blind. It has legs, it can run fast, it can move fast, but because it is blind it cannot choose the right direction in which to go. And it is bound to be continually stumbling, falling, hurting itself and feeling life meaningless. That's what the intellectuals of the whole world are saying: "Life is meaningless."

The reason why life seems to them meaningless is that the blind intellect is trying to see the light. It is impossible.

There is a heart within you, which sees, which feels, but which has no legs; it cannot run. It remains where it is, beating, waiting . . . someday intellect will understand and will be able to use the heart's eyes.

When I say the word *trust* I mean the eyes of the heart.

And when I say *doubt* I mean the legs of your intellect.

Both together can come out of the fire; there is no problem at all. But remember, the intellect has to accept the heart above its shoulders. It has to. The heart has no legs, only eyes, and intellect has to listen to the heart and follow its directions.

In the hands of the heart the intellect becomes intelligent. It is a transformation, a total transformation of energy. Then the person does not become an intellectual, he simply becomes wise.

Wisdom comes through the meeting of the heart and the intellect. And once you have learned the art of how to create a synchronicity between your heartbeats and the workings of your intellect, you have the whole secret in your hands, the master key to open all the mysteries.

## THE WAY OF INNOCENCE

The real question is not of courage, the real question is that the known is the dead, and the unknown is the living. Clinging to the known is clinging to a corpse. It does not need courage to drop the clinging; in fact, it needs courage to go on clinging to a corpse. You just have to see . . . That which is familiar to you, which you have lived—what has it given? Where have you reached? Are you not still empty? Is there not immense discontent, a deep frustration and meaninglessness? Somehow you go on managing, hiding the truth and creating lies to remain engaged, involved.

This is the question: to see with clarity that everything that you know is of the past, it is already gone. It is part of a graveyard. Do you want to be in a grave, or do you want to be alive? And this is not the question only today; it will be the same question tomorrow, and the day after tomorrow. It will be the same question at your last breath.

Whatever you know, accumulate—information, knowledge, experience—the moment you have explored them you are finished with them. Now carrying those empty words, that dead load, is crushing your life, burdening your life, preventing you from entering into a living, rejoicing being—which is awaiting you each moment.

The man of understanding dies every moment to the past and is reborn again to the future. His present is always a transformation, a rebirth, a resurrection. It is not a question of courage at all, that is the first thing to be understood. It is a question of clarity, of being clear about what is what.

And second, whenever there is really a question of courage, nobody can give it to you. It is not something that can be presented as a gift. It is something that you are born with, you just have not allowed it to grow, you have not allowed it to assert itself.

**INNOCENCE IS COURAGE AND CLARITY BOTH.** There is no need to have courage if you are innocent. There is no need, either, for any clarity because nothing can be more clear, crystal clear, than innocence. So the whole question is how to protect one's own innocence.

> In the hands of the heart the intellect becomes intelligent. It is a transformation, a total transformation of energy. Then the person does not become an intellectual, he simply becomes wise.

Innocence is not something to be achieved. It is not something to be learned. It is not something like a talent: painting, music, poetry, sculpture. It is not like those things. It is more like breathing, something you are born with.

Innocence is everybody's nature. Nobody is born other than innocent.

How can one be born other than innocent? Birth means you

have entered the world as a tabula rasa, nothing is written on you. You have only future, no past. That is the meaning of innocence. So first try to understand all the meanings of innocence.

The first is: no past, only future.

The past corrupts because it gives you memories, experiences, expectations. All those combined together make you clever but not clear. They make you cunning but not intelligent. They may help you to succeed in the world, but in your innermost being you will be a failure. And all the success of the world means nothing compared to the failure that finally you are going to face, because ultimately only your inner self remains with you. All is lost: your glory, your power, your name, your fame—all start disappearing like shadows.

> The man of understanding dies every moment to the past and is reborn again to the future. His present is always a transformation, a rebirth, a resurrection.

At the end only that remains which you had brought in the very beginning. You can take from this world only that which you have brought in.

In India it is common wisdom that the world is like a waiting room in a railway station; it is not your house. You are not going to remain in the waiting room forever. Nothing in the waiting room belongs to you—the furniture, the paintings on the wall. . . . You use them—you see the painting, you sit on the chair, you rest on the bed—but nothing belongs to you. You are just here for a few minutes, or for a few hours at the most, then you will be gone.

Yes, what you have brought in with you, into the waiting room, you will take away with you; that's yours. What have you brought into the world? And the world certainly is a waiting room. The waiting may not be in seconds, minutes, hours, days, it may be in years; but what does it matter whether you wait seven hours or seventy years?

You may forget, in seventy years, that you are just in a waiting room. You may start thinking perhaps you are the owner, perhaps this is the house you have built. You may start putting your nameplate on the waiting room.

There are people—I have seen it, because I was traveling so much: people have written their names in the bathrooms of the waiting room. People have engraved their names on the furniture of the waiting room. It looks stupid, but it is very similar to what people do in the world.

There is a very significant story in ancient Jaina scriptures. In India it is believed that if somebody can become the emperor of the whole world he is called a chakravartin. The word *chakra* means the "wheel." In ancient India it was a way to avoid unnecessary fighting and violence: a chariot, a golden chariot, very valuable, with beautiful and strong horses, would move from one kingdom to another kingdom. If the other kingdom did

> There is no need to have courage if you are innocent.
>
> There is no need, either, for any clarity because nothing can be more clear, crystal clear, than innocence.
>
> So the whole question is how to protect one's own innocence.

not resist and let the chariot pass, that meant that kingdom had accepted the owner of the chariot as its superior. Then there was no need to fight.

In this way the chariot would move, and wherever people obstructed the chariot then there would be war. If the chariot was not obstructed anywhere, then without any war the superiority of the king was proved: he became a chakravartin—one whose wheel has moved around and whom nobody has been able to obstruct. This has been the desire of all the kings, to become a chakravartin.

Certainly it needs more power than Alexander the Great had. Just to send your chariot . . . it needs tremendous power to support it. It needs the absolute certainty that if the chariot is obstructed there is going to be a mass slaughter. It means the man is recognized already, that if he wants to conquer anybody there is no way to prevent him conquering you.

> At the end only that remains which you had brought in the very beginning. You can take from this world only that which you have brought in.

But it is a very symbolic way, more civilized. There is no need to attack, there is no need to start killing; just send a symbolic message. So with the flag of the king the chariot will go, and if the other king feels that there is no point in resisting—that fighting simply means defeat and unnecessary violence, destruction—he welcomes the chariot, and in his capital flowers are thrown over the chariot.

This seems to be a far more civilized way than what countries like the Soviet Union and America are going to do. Just send a beautiful chariot—but that means your strength should be something absolutely certain to you; and not only to you, it should be certain to everybody else. Only then can such a symbol be of any help. So every king had the desire to become a chakravartin someday.

The story is that one man became a chakravartin—and it happens only once in thousands of years that a man becomes a chakravartin. Even Alexander the Great was not a world conqueror; there was yet much left unconquered. And he died very young, he was only thirty-three: there was not even time enough to conquer the world. What to say of conquering, the whole world was not even known! Half of the world was unknown, and the half that was known, even that was not conquered. This man, of whom I am going to tell you the story, became the chakravartin.

It is said that when a chakravartin dies—because a chakravartin happens only in thousands of years, he is a rare being—when he dies he is received in heaven with great rejoicing and he is taken to a special place.

In Jaina mythology, in heaven there is a parallel mountain to the Himalayas. The Himalayas are just made of rocks and earth and ice. The parallel to the Himalayas in heaven is called Sumeru. Sumeru means the ultimate mountain: nothing can be higher than that, nothing can be better than that. It is solid gold; instead of rocks there are diamonds and rubies and emeralds.

When a chakravartin dies he is led to Sumeru mountain to engrave his name on it. That is a rare opportunity; that happens only once in thousands of years. Of course this man was immensely excited that he was going to write his name on Sumeru. That is the ultimate catalog of all the great ones that have been, and will also be the catalog of all the great ones who are going to be. This emperor was becoming party to a lineage of supermen.

The gatekeeper gave him the instruments to engrave his name. He wanted to take a few of his men who had committed suicide just because their emperor was dying—they could not think of living without him. His wife, his prime minister, his commander in chief, all the great people who were around him had all committed suicide, so they had come with him.

The emperor wanted the gatekeeper to let them all come to see him engrave his name, because what is the joy if you go alone and engrave your name and nobody is there even to see?—because the real joy is that the whole world should see.

The gatekeeper said, "You listen to my advice, because this is my inherited profession. My father was a gatekeeper, his father was a gatekeeper; for centuries we have been gatekeepers to Sumeru mountain. Listen to my advice: Don't take them with you; otherwise you will repent."

The emperor could not understand, but neither could he ignore the advice—because what interest could that man have in preventing him?

The gatekeeper said, "If you still want them to see, first go engrave your name; then come back and take them with you if you want. I have no objection even now if you want to take them, but just in case you decide not to, then there will be no chance to change your mind . . . they will be with you. You go alone."

This was perfectly sane advice. The emperor said, "That's

good. I will go alone, engrave my name, come back, and call you all."

The gatekeeper said, "I am perfectly agreeable to that."

The emperor went and he saw the Sumeru shining under thousands of suns—because in heaven you cannot be so poor as to have just one sun—thousands of suns, and a golden mountain far bigger than the Himalayas—and the Himalayas are almost two thousand miles long! He could not open his eyes for a moment, it was so glaring there. And then he started looking for a space, the right space, but he was very much puzzled: there was no space; the whole mountain was engraved with names.

He could not believe his eyes. For the first time he became aware what he was. Up to now he was thinking he was a superman who happens once in thousands of years. But time has been from eternity; even thousands of years don't make any difference, so many chakravartins had happened already. There was no space on that biggest mountain in the whole universe where he could write his small name.

He came back, and now he understood that the gatekeeper was right not to take his wife and his commander in chief and his prime minister and other intimate friends. It was good that they had not seen the situation. They could still believe that their emperor was a rare being.

He took the gatekeeper aside and he said, "But there is no space!"

The gatekeeper said, "That's what I was telling you. What you have to do is to erase a few names and write down your name. That's what has been done; my whole life I have been seeing this done, my father used to say this has been done. My father's father—none of my family have seen Sumeru empty, or with any space, ever.

"Whenever a chakravartin has come he had to erase a few names and write his own name. So this is not the whole history of the chakravartins. Many times it has been erased, many times it has been engraved. You just do your work, and then if you want to show your friends you can bring them in."

The emperor said, "No, I don't want to show them and I don't want to even write my name. What is the point?—someday somebody will come and erase it.

"My whole life has become utterly meaningless. This was my only hope, that Sumeru, the golden mountain in heaven was going to have my name. For this I have lived, for this I have staked my life; for this I was ready to kill the whole world. And anybody else can erase my name and write his. What is the point of writing it? I will not write it."

The gatekeeper laughed.

The emperor said, "Why are you laughing?"

The gatekeeper said, "This is strange, because this too I have been hearing from my grandfathers—that chakravartins come, and seeing the whole story, just turn back; they don't write their names. You are not new: anybody having a little intelligence would do the same."

In this whole world what can you gain? What can you take away with you? Your name, your prestige, your respectability? Your money, your power—what? Your scholarship? You cannot take anything. Everything will have to be dropped here. And in that moment you will understand that all that you possessed was not yours; the very idea of possession was wrong. And because of that possession you were corrupted.

To increase that possession—to have more money, to have more power, to conquer more lands—you were doing things that even you cannot say were right. You were lying, you were dishonest. You were having hundreds of faces. You were not true even for a single moment to anybody or to yourself; you could not be. You had to be false, phony, pretending, because these are things that help you to succeed in the world. Authenticity is not going to help you. Honesty is not going to help you. Truthfulness is not going to help you.

Without possessions, success, fame—who are you? You don't know. You are your name, you are your fame, you are your prestige, your power. But other than these, who are you? So this whole possessiveness becomes your identity. It gives you a false sense of being. That's the ego.

Ego is not something mysterious, it is a very simple phenomenon. You don't know who you are, and to live without knowing who you are is impossible. If I don't know who I am, then what am I doing here? Then whatsoever I am doing becomes meaningless. The first and the foremost thing is to know who I am. Perhaps then I can do something that fulfills my nature, makes me contented, brings me home.

But if I don't know who I am, and I go on doing things, how can I manage to reach where my nature was supposed to reach, to lead? I have been running hither and thither, but there is not going to be any point that I can say, "Now I have arrived, this was the place I was searching for."

You don't know who you are, so some false identity is needed as a substitute. Your possessions give you that false identity.

You come with an innocent watcher into the world. Everybody comes in the same way, with the same quality of consciousness. But you start bargaining with the grown-up world. They have many things to give to you; you have only one thing to give, and that is your integrity, your self-respect. You don't have much, a single thing—you can call it anything: innocence, intelligence, authenticity. You have only one thing.

And the child is naturally very much interested in everything he sees around. He is continuously wanting to have this, to have that; that is part of human nature. If you look at the small child, even a just-born baby, you can see he has started groping for something; his hands are trying to find something. He has started the journey.

In the journey he will lose himself, because you can't get anything in this world without paying for it. And the poor child cannot understand that what he is giving is so valuable that if the whole world is on one side, and his integrity on the other side, then too his integrity will be more weighty, more valuable. The child has no way to know about it. This is the problem, because what he has got he has simply got. He takes it for granted.

Let me tell you one story that will make it clear.

One rich man, very rich, became in the end very frustrated, which is a natural outcome of all success. Nothing fails like success. Success is significant only if you are a failure. Once you succeed then you know that you have been cheated by the world, by the people, by the society. The man had all the riches but no peace of mind. He started looking for peace of mind.

That's what is happening in America. In America more people

are looking for peace of mind than anywhere else. In India I have never come across a person who is looking for peace of mind. Peace of the stomach has to be taken care of first—peace of mind is too far away. From the stomach the mind is almost millions of miles away.

But in America everybody is looking for peace of mind, and of course when you are looking for it, then people will be there ready to give it to you. This is a simple law of economics: wherever there is demand there is supply. It does not matter whether you really need what you are asking for. Nor does anybody bother about what the supply is going to give you—whether it is just bogus advertisement, propaganda, or whether there is something substantial.

Knowing this simple principle, that wherever there is demand there is supply, the cunning and clever people have gone one step ahead. Now they say, "There is no need to wait for demand to happen, you can create the demand." And that is the whole art of advertisement: it is creating demand.

> In America more people are looking for peace of mind than anywhere else. In India I have never come across a person who is looking for peace of mind. Peace of the stomach has to be taken care of first.

Before you read the advertisement you had no such demand, you had never felt that this was your need. But reading the advertisement, suddenly you feel, "My God, I have been missing it. And I am such a fool that I never knew that this thing exists."

Before somebody starts manufacturing something, producing something, even years ahead—three, four years ahead—he starts advertising. The thing is not there yet in the market because first the demand has to reach the minds of people. And once the demand is there, by that time the supply will be ready.

Bernard Shaw has said that when he was new and he published his first book, of course there was no demand—nobody had ever heard about George Bernard Shaw. How can you demand, "I want George Bernard Shaw's book, his drama"? So what he used to do the whole day . . . He published the book—he himself was the publisher, he put together the money himself—and then he went from one bookstore to another bookstore asking, "Have you got George Bernard Shaw's book?"

They said, "George Bernard Shaw? We never heard the name."

He said, "Strange, such a great man and you have never heard of him and you run a bookstore? Are you out-of-date or something? The first thing you should do is get George Bernard Shaw's book." He had published only one book, but he started advertising for several books, because when you are going around, why publicize just one book? And one book does not make a man a great writer.

He would go in different clothes—sometimes with a hat, sometimes with glasses. And people started calling at George Bernard Shaw's house. And he had to do all this—the advertising, supplying; that's how he sold his first book. He was asking people on the street, "Have you heard . . . because I am hearing so much about a certain book written by some George Bernard Shaw. People say it is just great, fantastic. Have you heard?"

They would say, "No, we have never even heard the name."

He said, "This is strange. I used to think London was a cultured society." And he went to libraries and clubs and everyplace where there was a possibility to create a demand, and he created the demand. He sold the book, and finally—that's what he was continuously doing—finally he became one of the greatest writers of this age. He had created the demand.

But if you succeed, there is no need for anybody to create the demand for peace of mind. If you succeed, you lose peace of mind on the way. That is a natural course. Success takes all peace from your mind. It simply sucks everything that is significant in life: peace, silence, joy, love. It goes on taking everything away from you. Finally your hands are full of junk, and all that was valuable is lost. And suddenly you realize peace of mind is needed.

Immediately there are suppliers, who don't know anything about mind, who don't know anything about peace. I have read one book entitled *Peace of Mind* by a Jewish rabbi, Joshua Liebman. I have gone through the whole book; the man knows neither about peace nor does he know about the mind. But he is a businessman. He has done a good job without knowing anything about peace of mind.

His book is one of the best sellers in the world because whoever wants peace of mind is bound to sooner or later find Joshua Liebman's book. And he has written it beautifully. He is a good writer, very articulate, impressive; you will be influenced by it. But peace of mind will remain as far away as it was before, or it may even have gone farther away by your reading this book.

In fact, if a man knows what peace is, and what mind is, he cannot write a book entitled *Peace of Mind*, because mind is the cause of all unpeace, all restlessness. Peace is when there is no mind.

So peace of mind—no commodity like this exists. If mind is there, then peace is not. If peace is there, then mind is not. But to write a book "Peace of No Mind"—nobody is going to purchase it. I have been thinking . . . but I thought, nobody is going to purchase "Peace of No Mind." It just will not make sense to them, but that's exactly the truth.

The child is unaware of what he has brought with him. This rich man was in the same position. He had all the riches in the world, and now he was searching for peace of mind. He went from one sage to another and they all gave great advice, but advice helps nobody.

In fact, only fools give advice, and only fools take advice. Wise people are very reluctant to give you advice because a wise man certainly knows that the only thing in the world which is given freely is advice, and that which is never taken by anybody is advice, so why should he bother?

A wise man first prepares you so that you can take the advice. He does not simply give you advice; you need to be prepared. It may take years to prepare you, to prepare the ground, and only then can you sow the seeds. It will be a fool who simply goes on throwing seeds on rocks and stones without even bothering that he is wasting seeds.

All these sages gave him advice, but nothing clicked. Finally a man whom he had not asked, who was not in any way a famous man—on the contrary, he was thought to be the village idiot—that man stopped him on the road one day and said, "You are unnecessarily wasting your time. None of these are sages; I know them perfectly, but because I am an idiot nobody believes me. Perhaps you will also not believe me, but I know a sage.

"Just seeing you so tortured continuously for peace of mind, I thought it would be better if I showed you the right person. Otherwise I am an idiot; nobody asks me for advice and I never give any advice to anybody. But it was too much: seeing you so sad and so miserable, I broke my silence. You go to this man in the next village."

The rich man immediately went, with a big bag full of precious diamonds, on his beautiful horse. He reached there, he saw that man—this man was known to the Sufis as Mulla Nasruddin.

He asked the Mulla, "Can you help me to attain peace of mind?"

Mulla said, "Help? I can give it to you."

The rich man thought, "This is strange. First that idiot suggested . . . and just out of desperation I thought there is no harm, so I came here. This seems to be even a greater idiot: he is saying, 'I can give it to you.' "

The rich man said, "You can give it to me? I have been to all kinds of sages; they all give advice—do this, do that, discipline yourself, do charity, help the poor, open hospitals, this and that. They say all these things, and in fact I have done all those things; nothing helps. In fact, more and more trouble arises. And you say you can give it to me?"

> If a man knows what peace is, and what mind is, he cannot write a book entitled *Peace of Mind*, because mind is the cause of all unpeace, all restlessness.
> Peace is when there is no mind.
> So peace of mind—no commodity like this exists.

The Mulla said, "It is so simple. You get down from the horse." So the rich man got down from the horse. He was holding his bag, and Mulla asked, "What are you holding in your bag so closely to your heart?"

He said, "These are precious diamonds. If you can give me peace, I will give you this bag." But before he could even figure out what was happening, Mulla took the bag and ran away!

The rich man, for a moment, was in shock; he could not even understand what to do. And then he had to follow him. But it was Mulla's own town—he knew every street and shortcut, and he was running. The rich man had never run in his whole life and he was so fat. . . . He was crying and huffing and puffing, and tears were rolling down. He said, "I have been completely cheated! This man has taken away all my life's hard work, my earnings; everything he has taken away."

So a crowd followed, and all were laughing. He said, "Are you all idiots? Is this town full of idiots? I have been completely ruined, and rather than catching hold of the thief you are all laughing."

They said, "He is not a thief, he is a very sage man."

The rich man said, "That idiot from my village got me into this trouble!" But somehow, running, perspiring, he followed Mulla. Mulla arrived back under the same tree where the horse was still standing. He sat down under the tree with the bag, and the rich man came crying and weeping. Mulla said, "You take this bag." The rich man took the bag and put it close to his heart. Mulla said, "How does it feel? Can you feel some peace of mind?"

The rich man said, "Yes it feels very peaceful. You are a strange man, and you have strange methods."

Mulla said, "No strange methods—simple mathematics. Whatever you have, you start taking it for granted. You just have to be given an opportunity to lose it; then immediately you will become aware of what you have lost. You have not gained anything new; it is the same bag that you have been carrying with no peace of mind. Now you are holding the same bag close to your heart and anybody can see how peaceful you are looking, a perfect sage! Just go home and don't bother people."

This is the problem for the child, because he comes with innocence, and he is ready to buy anything and give his innocence. He is ready to buy any rubbish and give his courage. He is ready to buy just toys—and what else is there in this world except toys?—and lose his clarity. He will understand only when all these toys are there in his possession and he can't feel any joy from them, can't see any achievement, any fulfillment. Then he becomes aware of what he has lost—and he himself has lost it.

In a better world, every family will learn from children. You are in such a hurry to teach them. Nobody seems to learn from them, and they have much to teach you. And you have nothing to teach them.

Just because you are older and powerful you start making them just like you without ever thinking about what you are, where you have reached, what your status is in the inner world. You are a pauper; and you want the same for your child also?

But nobody thinks; otherwise people would learn from small children. Children bring so much from the other world because they are such fresh arrivals. They still carry the silence of the womb, the silence of the very existence.

ALWAYS REMEMBER, TRUST IN THE UNKNOWN. The known is the mind. The unknown cannot be the mind. It may be something else but it cannot be the mind. One thing certain about the mind is that mind is the accumulated known. So, for example, if you come across a fork in the road and the mind says, "Go this way, this is familiar"—that is the mind. If you listen to your being, it would like to go to the unfamiliar, to the unknown. The being is always an adventurer. The mind is very orthodox, very conservative. It wants to move into the track, the trodden path, again and again—the path of least resistance.

> In a better world, every family will learn from children. You are in such a hurry to teach them. Nobody seems to learn from them, and they have much to teach you.

So always listen for the unknown. And gather courage to move into the unknown.

To grow to your destiny needs great courage, it needs fearlessness. People who are full of fear cannot move beyond the known. The known gives a kind of comfort, security, safety because it is known. One is perfectly aware, one knows how to deal with it. One can remain almost asleep and go on dealing with it—there is no need to be awake; that's the convenience with the known.

The moment you cross the boundary of the known, fear arises, because now you will be ignorant, now you will not know what to do, what not to do. Now you will not be so sure of yourself, now mistakes can be committed; you can go astray. That is the fear that keeps people tethered to the known, and once a person is tethered to the known, he is dead.

Life can only be lived dangerously—there is no other way to live it. It is only through danger that life attains to maturity, growth. One needs to be an adventurer, always ready to risk the known for the unknown. And once one has tasted the joys of freedom and fearlessness, one never repents because then one knows what it means to live at the optimum. Then one knows what it means to burn your life's torch from both ends together. And even a single moment of that intensity is more gratifying than the whole eternity of mediocre living.

# WHEN THE NEW KNOCKS ON YOUR DOOR, OPEN IT!

*The new is unfamiliar. It may be the friend, it may be the enemy, who knows? And there is no way to know! The only way to know is to allow it; hence the apprehension, the fear.*

The new does not arise out of you, it comes from the beyond. It is not part of you. Your whole past is at stake. The new is discontinuous with you, hence the fear. You have lived in one way, you have thought in one way, you have made a comfortable life out of your beliefs. Then something new knocks on the door. Now your whole past pattern is going to be disturbed. If you allow the new to enter, you will never be the same again; the new will transform you.

It is risky. One never knows where you will end with the new. The old is known, familiar; you have lived with it for long, you are acquainted with it. The new is unfamiliar. It may be the friend, it may be the enemy, who knows? And there is no way to know! The only way to know is to allow it; hence the apprehension, the fear.

And you cannot keep rejecting it either, because the old has not given you yet what you seek. The old has been promising, but the promises have not been fulfilled. The old is familiar but miserable. The new is maybe going to be uncomfortable but there is a possibility—it may bring bliss to you. So you cannot reject it and you cannot accept it either; hence you waver, you tremble, great anguish arises in your being. It is natural, nothing has gone wrong. This is how it has always been, this is how it will always be.

Try to understand the appearance of the new. Everybody in the world wants to become new, because nobody is satisfied with the old. Nobody can ever be satisfied with the old because whatsoever it is, you have known it. Once known it has become repetitive; once known it has become boring, monotonous. You want to get rid of it. You want to explore, you want to adventure. You want to become new, and yet when the new knocks on the door, you shrink back, you withdraw, you hide in the old. This is the dilemma.

How do we become new?—and everybody wants to become new. Courage is needed, and not ordinary courage; extraordinary courage is needed. And the world is full of cowards, hence people have stopped growing. How can you grow if you are a coward? With each new opportunity you shrink back, you close your eyes. How can you grow? How can you be? You only pretend to be.

And because you cannot grow you have to find substitute growths. You cannot grow, but your bank balance can grow—that's a substitute. It needs no courage, it is perfectly adjusted with your cowardliness. Your bank balance goes on growing and you start thinking that you are growing. You become more respectable. Your name and fame go on growing and you think you are growing? You are simply deceiving yourself. Your name is not you, neither is your fame you. Your bank balance is not your being. But if you think of the being you start shaking, because if you want to grow there then you have to drop all cowardice.

How do we become new? We do not become new of ourselves. Newness comes from the beyond, say from God. Newness comes from existence. Mind is always old. Mind is never new; it is the accumulation of the past. Newness comes from the beyond; it is a gift from God. It is from the beyond and it is of the beyond.

The unknown and the unknowable, the beyond, has ingress into you. It has ingress into you because you are never sealed and set apart; you are not an island. You may have forgotten the beyond but the beyond has not forgotten you. The child may have forgotten the mother, the mother has not forgotten the child. The part may have started thinking, "I am separate," but the whole knows that you are not separate. The whole has ingress in you. It is still in contact with you. That's why the new goes on coming, although you don't welcome it. It comes every morning, it comes every evening. It comes in a thousand and one ways. If you have eyes to see, you will see it continuously coming to you.

> You are not an island. You may have forgotten the beyond, but the beyond has not forgotten you. The child may have forgotten the mother, the mother has not forgotten the child. The part may have started thinking, "I am separate," but the whole knows that you are not separate.

Existence goes on showering on you, but you are enclosed in your past. You are almost in a kind of grave. You have become insensitive. Because of your cowardliness you have lost your sensitivity. To be sensitive means the new will be felt—and the thrill of the new, and the passion for the new and the adventure will arise and you will start moving into the unknown, not knowing where you are going.

Mind thinks it is mad. Mind thinks it is not rational to leave the old. But God is always the new. That's why we cannot use past tense or future tense for God. We cannot say "God was," we cannot say "God will be." We can only use the present: "God is." It is always fresh, virgin. And it has ingress in you.

Remember, anything new coming in your life is a message from God. If you accept it you are religious. If you reject it you are irreligious. Man needs just to relax a little more to accept the new; to open up a little more to let the new in. Give way to God entering you.

That is the whole meaning of prayer or meditation—you open up, you say yes, you say, "Come in." You say, "I have been waiting and waiting and I am thankful that you have come." Always receive the new with great joy. Even if sometimes the new leads you into inconvenience, still it is worth it. Even if sometimes the new leads you into some ditch, still it is worth it, because only through errors one learns, and only through difficulties one grows. The new will bring difficulties. That's why you choose the old—it does not bring any difficulties. It is a consolation, it is a shelter.

And only the new, accepted deeply and totally, can transform you. You cannot bring the new in your life; the new *comes*. You can either accept it or reject it. If you reject it you remain a stone, closed and dead. If you receive it you become a flower, you start opening . . . and in that opening is celebration.

Only the entry of the new can transform you, there is no other way of transformation. And remember, it has nothing to do with you and your efforts. But to do nothing is not to cease to act; it is to act without will or direction or impulse from your past. The search for the new cannot be an ordinary search, because it is for the new—how can you search for it? You don't know it, you have never met it. The search for the new is going to be just an open exploration. One knows not. One has to start in a state of not knowing, and one has to move innocently like a child, thrilled with the possibilities— and infinite are the possibilities.

You cannot bring the new in your life, the new comes. You can either accept it or reject it.

You cannot do anything to create the new, because whatsoever you do will be of the old, will be from the past. But that does not mean that you have to cease to act. It is to act without will or direction or impulse from your past. Act without any will or direction or impulse from the past—and that is to act meditatively. Act spontaneously. Let the moment be decisive.

You don't impose your decision, because the decision will be from the past and it will destroy the new. You just act in the moment like a child. Utterly abandon yourself to the moment—and you will find every day new openings, new light, new insight. And those new insights will go on changing you. One day, suddenly you will see you are each moment new. The old no more lingers, the old no more hangs around you like a cloud. You are like a dewdrop, fresh and young.

That is the real meaning of resurrection. If you understand this you will be free from memory—psychological memory, that is. Memory is a dead thing. Memory is not truth and cannot ever be, because truth is always alive, truth is life; memory is persistence of that which is no more. It is living in a ghost world, but it contains us, it is our prison. In fact, it is us. Memory creates the knot, the complex called "I," the ego. And naturally this false entity called "I" is continuously afraid of death. That's why you are afraid of the new.

This "I" is afraid, not really you. The being has no fear, but the ego has fear, because the ego is very very afraid of dying. It is artificial, it is ar-bitrary, it is put together. It can fall apart any moment. And when the new enters, there is fear. The ego is afraid, it may fall apart. Somehow it has been managing to keep itself together, to keep itself in one piece, and now something new comes—it will be a shattering thing. That's why you don't accept the new with joy. The ego cannot accept its own death with joy—how can it accept its own death with joy?

> You just act in the moment like a child. Utterly abandon yourself to the moment—and you will find every day new openings, new light, new insight. And those new insights will go on changing you.

Unless you have understood that you are not the ego, you will not be able to receive the new. Once you have seen that the ego is your past memory and nothing else, that you are not your memory, that memory is just like a biocomputer, that it is a machine, a mechanism, utilitarian, but you are beyond it . . . you are consciousness, not memory. Memory is a content in consciousness, you are consciousness itself.

For example, you see somebody walking on the road. You remember the face but you can't remember the name. If you are the memory you should remember the name too. But you say, "I recognize the face but I don't remember the name." Then you start looking in your memory, you go inside your memory, you look to this side, to that side, and suddenly the name bubbles up and you say, "Yes, this is his name." Memory is your record. You are the one who is looking into the record, you are not the memory itself.

And it happens many times that if you become too tense about remembering something it becomes difficult to remember it, because the very tension, the very strain upon your being does not allow the memory to release its information to you. You try and try to remember somebody's name and it doesn't come, even though you say it is just on the tip of the tongue. You know that you know, but still the name is not coming.

Now this is strange. If you are memory, then who is preventing you and how is it not coming? And who is this who says, "I know, but still it is not coming"? And then you try hard, and the harder you try the more difficult it becomes. Then, fed up with the whole thing, you go into the garden for a walk and suddenly, looking at the rosebush, it is there, it has surfaced.

Your memory is not you. You are consciousness, memory is content. But memory is the whole life energy of the ego. Memory is of course old, and it is afraid of the new. The new may be disturbing, the new may be such that it may not be digestible. The new may bring some trouble. You will have to shift and reshift yourself. You will have to readjust yourself. That seems arduous.

To be new one needs to become disidentified with the ego. Once you are disidentified with the ego you don't care whether it dies or lives. In fact, you know that whether it lives or dies, it is already dead. It is just a mechanism. Use it but don't be used by it. The ego is continuously afraid of death because it is arbitrary, hence the fear. It does not arise out of being; it cannot arise out of being, because being is life—how can life be afraid of death? Life knows nothing of death. The ego arises out of the arbitrary, the artificial, the somehow put together, the false, the pseudo. And it is just such letting go, just that death of the ego, that makes a man alive. To die in the ego is to be born into *being*.

> Your memory is not you. You are consciousness, memory is content. But memory is the whole life energy of the ego.

The new is a messenger from God, the new is a message from God. It is a gospel! Listen to the new, go with the new. I know you are afraid. In spite of the fear, go with the new, and your life will become richer and richer and you will be able one day to release your imprisoned splendor.

WE GO ON MISSING MANY THINGS in life just because we lack courage. In fact, no effort is needed to achieve—just courage—and things start coming to you rather than you going to them . . . at least in the inner world it is so.

And to me, to be blissful is the greatest courage. To be miserable is very cowardly. In fact to be miserable, nothing is needed. Any coward can do it, any fool can do it. Everybody is capable of being miserable, but to be blissful, great courage is needed—it is an uphill task.

Ordinarily we don't think so—we think, "What is needed to be happy? Everybody wants to be happy." That is absolutely wrong. Very rarely does a person want to be happy—notwithstanding what they go on saying. Very rarely is a person ready to be happy—people have so much investment in their misery. They love to be unhappy . . . in fact they are happy in being unhappy.

There are many things to be understood—otherwise it is very difficult to get out of the rut of misery. The first thing: that nobody is holding you there; it is you who has decided to remain in that prison of misery. Nobody holds anybody. A man who is ready to

> Very rarely does a person want to be happy—notwithstanding what they go on saying. Very rarely is a person ready to be happy—people have so much investment in their misery. They love to be unhappy . . . in fact they are happy in being unhappy.

get out of it, can get out of it right this very moment. Nobody else is responsible. If one is miserable, one is responsible, but a miserable person never accepts the responsibility—that is his way of remaining miserable. He says, "Somebody else is making me miserable."

If somebody else is making you miserable, naturally, what can you do? If you are making yourself miserable, something can be done . . . something can be done immediately. Then it is within your hands to be or not to be miserable. So people go on throwing the responsibility—sometimes on the wife, sometimes on the husband, sometimes on the family, sometimes on the conditioning, the childhood, the mother, the father . . . sometimes the society, the history, fate, God, but they always go on throwing. The names are different, but the trick is the same.

> A man really becomes a man when he accepts total responsibility—he is responsible for whatsoever he is. This is the first courage, the greatest courage.

A man really becomes a man when he accepts total responsibility—he is responsible for whatsoever he is. This is the first courage, the greatest courage. Very difficult to accept it, because the mind goes on saying, "If you are responsible, why do you create it?" To avoid this we say that somebody else is responsible: "What can I do? I am helpless . . . I am a victim! I am being tossed from here and there by greater forces than me and I cannot do anything. So at the most I can cry about being miserable and become more miserable by crying." And everything grows—if you practice it, it grows. Then you go deeper and deeper . . . you sink in deeper and deeper.

Nobody, no other force, is doing anything to you. It is you and only you. This is the whole philosophy of karma—that it is your doing; *karma* means doing. You have done it and you can undo it. And there is no need to wait, to delay. Time is not needed—you can simply jump out of it!

But we have become habituated. We will feel very lonely if we stop being miserable, we will lose our closest companion. It has become our shadow—it follows us everywhere. When nobody is there at least your misery is with you—one is married to it. And it is a long, long marriage; you have remained married to misery for many lives.

Now the time has come to divorce it. That I call the great courage—to divorce misery, to lose the oldest habit of the human mind, the longest companion.

# THE COURAGE
# OF LOVE

*Fear is nothing but absence of love. Do something with love,
forget about fear. If you love well, fear disappears.*

I f you love deeply, fear is not found. Fear is a negativity, an
absence. This has to be understood very, very deeply. If you
miss there, you will never be able to understand the nature of
fear. It is like darkness. Darkness does not exist, it only appears to
be. In fact it is just an absence of light. Light exists; remove the
light—there is darkness.

Darkness does not exist, you cannot remove darkness. Do
whatsoever you want to do, you cannot remove darkness. You
cannot bring it, you cannot throw it. If you want to do something with darkness, you will have to do something with light,
because only something that has an existence can be related to. Put
the light off, darkness is there; put the light on, darkness is not
there—but you do something with *light*. You cannot do anything
with darkness.

Fear is darkness. It is absence of love. You cannot do anything
about it, and the more you do, the more you will become fearful
because then the more you will find it impossible. The problem
will become more and more complicated. If you fight with dark-

ness, you will be defeated. You can bring a sword and try to kill the darkness: you will only be exhausted. And finally the mind will think, "Darkness is so powerful, that's why I am defeated."

This is where logic goes wrong. It is absolutely logical—if you have been struggling with darkness and you could not defeat it, could not destroy it, it is absolutely logical to come to the conclusion that "darkness is very, very powerful. I am impotent before it." But the reality is just the opposite. You are not impotent; darkness is impotent. In fact darkness is not there—that's why you could not defeat it. How can you defeat something which is not?

Don't fight with the fear; otherwise you will become more and more afraid and a new fear will enter into your being: that is fear of fear, which is very dangerous. In the first place fear is an absence, and in the second place the fear of fear is the fear of the absence of absence. Then you go into a madness!

Fear is nothing but absence of love. Do something with love, forget about fear. If you love well, fear disappears. If you love deeply, fear is not found.

Whenever you have been in love with someone, even for a single moment, was there any fear? It has never been found in any relationship where, if even for a single moment, two persons are in deep love and a meeting happens, they are tuned to each other—in that moment fear has never been found. Just as if the light is on and darkness has not been found—there is the secret key: love more.

If you feel there is fear in your being, love more. Be courageous in love, take courage. Be adventurous in love; love more, and love unconditionally, because the more you love the less will be the fear.

And when I say love I mean all the four layers of love, from sex to samadhi.

Love deeply.

If you love deeply in a sexual relationship much fear will disappear from the body. If your body trembles in fear, it is the fear of sex; you have not been in a deep sexual relationship. Your body trembles, your body is not at ease, at home.

Love deeply—a sexual orgasm will dispel all fear out of the body. When I say it will dispel all fear I don't mean that you will become brave, because brave people are nothing but cowards upside down. When I say all fear will disappear I mean there will be no cowardice and no bravery. Those are two aspects of fear.

Look at your brave people: you will find that deep inside they are afraid, they have just created an armor around them. Bravery is not fearlessness; it is fear well protected, well defended, armored.

> If your body trembles in fear, it is the fear of sex; you have not been in a deep sexual relationship. Your body trembles, your body is not at ease, at home.

When fear disappears you become fearless. And a fearless person is one who never creates fear in anybody and who never allows anybody to create fear in him.

Deep sexual orgasm gives the body at-homeness. A very, very deep health happens in the body because the body feels whole.

Then the second step is love. Love people—unconditionally.

If you have some conditions in the mind then you will never be able to love; those conditions will become barriers. Because love is beneficial to you, why bother about conditions? It is so beneficial, it is such a deep well-being—love unconditionally, don't ask anything in return. If you can come to understand that just by loving people you grow in fearlessness, you will love for the sheer joy of it!

Ordinarily people love only when their conditions are fulfilled. They say, You should be like this, only then will I love. A mother says to the child, "I'll love you only if you behave." A wife says to the husband, "You have to be *this* way, only then can I love you." Everybody creates conditions; love disappears.

Love is an infinite sky! You cannot force it into narrow spaces, conditioned, limited. If you bring fresh air into your house and close it off from everywhere—all the windows closed, all the doors closed—soon it becomes stale. Whenever love happens it is a part of freedom; then soon you bring that fresh air into your house and everything goes stale, dirty.

This is a deep problem for the whole of humanity—it has been a problem. When you fall in love everything looks beautiful, because in those moments you don't put conditions. Two persons move near each other unconditionally. Once they have settled, once they have started taking each other for granted, then conditions are being imposed: "You should be like this, you should behave like that, only then will I love"—as if love is a bargain.

When you don't love out of your fullness of heart, you are bargaining. You want to force the other person to do something for you, only then will you love; otherwise you will betray your love. Now you are using your love as a punishment, or as an en-

forcement, but you are not loving. Either you are trying to with-
hold your love or you are giving your love, but in both cases love
in itself is not the end, something else is.

If you are a husband then you bring presents to the wife—she
is happy, she clings to you, kisses you; but when you don't bring
anything to the house there is a distance; she does not cling, she
does not come near to you. When you do such things you are
forgetting that when you love it is beneficial to you, not only to
others. In the first place love helps those who love. In the second
place it helps those who are being loved.

People come to me, they always say, "The other is not loving
me." Nobody comes and says, "I am not loving the other." Love
has become a demand: "The other is not loving me." Forget about
the other! Love is such a beautiful phenomenon, if *you* love you
will enjoy.

And the more you love, the more you become lovable. The
less you love and the more you demand that others should love
you, the less and less you are lovable, the more and more
you become closed, confined to your ego. And you become
touchy—even if somebody approaches you to love you, you become afraid, because in every love there is a possibility of rejection,
withdrawal.

Nobody loves you—this has become an ingrained thought
within you. How is this man trying to change your mind? He is
trying to love *you?* Must be something false, is he trying to deceive
you? Must be a cunning man, tricky. You protect yourself. You
don't allow anybody to love you and you don't love others. Then
there is fear. Then you are alone in the world, so alone, so lonely,
not connected.

What is fear, then? Fear is a feeling of no contact with existence. Let this be the definition of fear: a state of no contact with existence is fear. You are left alone, a child crying in the house, the mother and father and the whole family gone to the theater. The child cries and weeps in his cradle. Left alone with no contact, nobody to protect, nobody to give solace, nobody to love; a loneliness, a vast loneliness all around. This is the state of fear.

> Fear is a feeling of no contact with existence.
> Let this be the definition of fear: a state of no contact with existence is fear.

This comes up because you are brought up in such a way that you don't allow love to happen. The whole of humanity has been trained for other things, not for love. To kill, we have been trained. And armies exist, years of training to kill! To calculate, we have been trained; colleges, universities exist, years of training just to calculate so that nobody can deceive you, but you can deceive others. But nowhere is there any opportunity available where you are allowed to love—and love in freedom.

In fact, not only that, the society hinders every effort to love. Parents don't like their children to fall in love. No father likes it, no mother likes it; whatsoever their pretensions no father, no mother, likes their children to fall in love. They like arranged marriage.

Why? Because once a young man falls in love with a woman or a girl, he is moving away from the family; he is creating a new family, his own family. He is against the old family of course, he is rebellious, he is saying, "Now I am going away, I will create my own home." And he chooses his own woman; the father has nothing to do with it, the mother has nothing to do with it, they seem completely cut off.

No, they would like to arrange it: "You create a home, but let us arrange it so we have some say in it. And don't fall in love—because when you fall in love, the love becomes the whole world." If it is an arranged marriage it is just a social affair; you are not in love, your wife is not your whole world, your husband is not your whole world. So wherever arranged marriage continues, the family continues. And wherever love marriage has come into being, the family is disappearing.

In the West the family is disappearing. Now you can see the whole logic of why there is arranged marriage: the family wants to exist. If you are destroyed, if your very possibility of love is destroyed, that is not the point; you have to be sacrificed for the family. If a marriage is arranged then a joint family exists. Then in a family a hundred persons can live—if marriage is arranged. But if some boy falls in love or some girl falls in love, then they become a world unto themselves. They want to move alone, they want their privacy. They don't want a hundred people around, uncles and uncles' uncles and cousins' cousins . . . they don't want this whole market around; they would like to have their own private world. This whole thing seems to be disturbing.

The family is against love. You must have heard that the family is the source of love, but I tell you: family is against love. Family has existed by killing love, it has not allowed love to happen.

The society does not allow love because if a person is really in deep love he cannot be manipulated. You cannot send him to war; he will say, "I am so happy where I am! Where are you sending me? And why should I go and kill strangers who may be happy in their homes? And we have no conflict, no clash of interests. . . ."

If the young generation moves deeper and deeper in love, wars will disappear because you will not be able to find enough mad people to go to the war. If you love, you have tasted something of life; you would not like death and killing people. When you don't love you have not tasted something of life; you love death.

Fear kills, wants to kill. Fear is destructive; love is a creative energy. When you love you would like to create—you may like to sing a song, or paint, or create poetry, but you would not take a bayonet or an atom bomb and go rushing off madly to kill people who are absolutely unknown to you, who have done nothing, who are as unknown to you as you are unknown to them.

The world will drop wars only when love enters into the world again. Politicians don't want you to love, the society does not want you to love, the family doesn't allow you to love. They all want to control your love energy because that is the only energy there is. That's why there is fear.

If you understand me well, drop all fears and love more—and love unconditionally. Don't think that you are doing something for the other when you love; you are doing something *for yourself*. When you love it is beneficial to you. So don't wait; don't say that when others love, you will love—that is not the point at all.

Be selfish. Love is selfish. Love people—you will be fulfilled through it, you will be getting more and more blessedness through it.

And when love goes deeper, fear disappears; love is the light, fear is darkness.

And then there is the third stage of love—prayer. Churches, religions, organized sects—they teach you to pray. But in fact they hinder you from praying because prayer is a spontaneous phenomenon, it cannot be taught. If you have been taught a prayer in your childhood, you have been prevented from a beautiful experience that could have happened. Prayer is a spontaneous phenomenon.

I must tell you one story I love. Leo Tolstoy has written a small story: In a certain part of old Russia there was a lake, and it became famous because of three saints. The whole country became interested. Thousands of people were going and journeying to the lake to see those three saints.

The high priest of the country became afraid: What is happening? He had never heard of these "saints"

> Be selfish.
> Love is selfish.
> Love people—you will be fulfilled through it, you will be getting more and more blessedness through it.
> And when love goes deeper, fear disappears; love is the light, fear is darkness.

and they had not been certified by the church; who has made them saints? This Christianity has been doing—one of the most foolish things—they give certificates: "This man is a saint." As if you can make a man a saint by certifying him!

But the people were going wild, and much news was coming that miracles were happening, so the priest had to go and see what the situation was. He went in a boat to the island where those three poor people lived; they were simply poor people, but very happy—because there is only one poverty and that poverty is a heart that cannot love. They were poor, but they were rich, the richest you could ever find.

They were happy sitting under a tree laughing, enjoying, delighting. Seeing the priest they bowed down, and the priest said, "What are you doing here? There are rumors that you are great saints. Do you know how to pray?"—because seeing these three persons the priest could immediately sense that they were completely uneducated, a little idiotic—happy, but foolish.

So they looked at each other and they said, "Sorry sir, we don't know the right prayer authorized by the church because we are ignorant. But we have created one prayer of our own—it is homemade. If you won't feel offended we can show it to you."

So the priest said, "Yes, show it to me, what prayer you are doing." So they said, "We tried and thought and thought—but we are not great thinkers, we are foolish people, ignorant villagers. Then we decided upon a simple prayer. In Christianity God is thought of as a trinity, three: God the Father, the Son, and the Holy Ghost. And we are also three. So we decided on a prayer: 'You are three, we are three, have mercy upon us.' This is our prayer: 'We are three, you are also three, have mercy on us.' "

The priest was very, very angry, almost enraged. He said, "What nonsense! We have never heard any prayer like this. Stop it! This way you cannot be saints. You are simply stupid." They fell at his feet and they said, "You teach us the real, the authentic prayer."

So he told them the authorized version of the prayer of the Russian Orthodox church. It was long, complicated, big words, bombastic. Those three persons looked at each other—it seemed impossible, the door of heaven was closed for them. They said, "You please tell us once more, because it is long, and we are un-educated." He said it again. They said, "Once more sir, because we will forget, and something will go wrong." So again he told it. They thanked him heartily, and he felt very good that he had done a good deed and brought three foolish people back to the church.

He sailed off in his boat. Just in the middle of the lake he could not believe his eyes—those three persons, those foolish people, were coming running on the water! They said, "Wait . . . once more . . . we have forgotten!"

Now this was impossible to believe! The priest fell at their feet and he said, "Forgive me. You continue your prayer."

The third love energy is prayer. Religions, organized churches, have destroyed it. They have given you ready-made prayers. Prayer is a spontaneous feeling. Remember this story when you pray. Let your prayer be a spontaneous phenomenon. If even your prayer cannot be spontaneous, then what will be? If even with God you have to be ready-made, then where will you be authentic and true and natural?

Say things that you would like to say. Talk to God as you would talk to a wise friend. But don't bring formalities in. A formal relationship is not a relationship at all. And you have become formal with God also? You miss all spontaneousness.

Bring love into prayer. Then you can talk! It is a beautiful thing, a dialogue with the universe.

But have you watched? If you are really spontaneous, people will think you are mad. If you go to a tree and start talking, or to a flower, a rose, people will think you are mad. If you go to the church and talk to the cross or to an image, nobody will think you are mad, they will think you are religious. You are talking to a stone in the temple and everybody thinks you are religious because this is the authorized form.

If you talk to a rose, which is more alive than any stone image, which is more divine than any stone image . . . If you talk to a tree, which is more deeply rooted in God than any cross because no cross has roots, it is a dead thing—that's why it kills . . . A tree is alive, with roots deep into the earth, branches high into the sky, connected with the whole, with the rays of the sun, with the stars— talk to the trees! That can be a contact point with the divine.

But if you talk that way people will think you are mad. Spontaneousness is thought to be madness. Formalities are thought to be sanity. Just the opposite is the reality. When you go into a temple and you simply repeat some memorized prayer, you are simply foolish. Have a heart-to-heart talk! And prayer is beautiful, you will start flowering through it.

Prayer is to be in love—to be in love with the whole. And sometimes you get angry with the whole and you don't talk; that's beautiful! You say, "I will not talk, enough is enough, and you have not been listening to me!" A beautiful gesture, not dead. And sometimes you drop praying completely, because you go on praying and God is not listening. It is a relationship with deep involvement in it, you get angry. Sometimes you feel very good, feel thankful, grateful; sometimes you feel put off. But let it be a *living* relationship. Then prayer is true. If you just go on like a gramophone and repeat the same thing every day, it is not prayer.

I have heard about a lawyer who was a very calculating man. Every night he would go to bed, look at the sky and say, "Ditto. Just like the other days," and go to sleep. Only once he prayed—the first time in his life—and then, "Ditto." It was like a legal thing; what was the point in saying the same prayer again? Whether you say ditto or you repeat the whole thing, it is the same.

Prayer should be a lived experience, a heart-to-heart dialogue. And soon, if it is heartful, you will feel that not only are you talking but the response is there. Then prayer has come into its own, come of age. When you feel the response, that not only you are talking—if it is a monologue it is still not prayer—it becomes a dialogue. You not only speak, you listen.

And I tell you the whole existence is ready to respond. Once your heart is open the whole responds.

There is nothing like prayer. No love can be as beautiful as prayer. Just as no sex can be as beautiful as love, no love can be as beautiful as prayer.

But then there is the fourth stage, which I call meditation. There, dialogue also ceases. Then you have a dialogue in silence. Words drop, because when the heart is really full you cannot speak. When the heart is too overflowing only silence can be the medium. Then there is no "other." You are one with the universe. You neither say anything nor listen to anything. You *are* with the one, with the universe, with the whole. A oneness—this is meditation.

These are the four stages of love, and on each stage there will be a disappearance of fear. If sex happens beautifully, the body fear will disappear. The body will not be neurotic. Ordinarily—I have observed thousands of bodies—they are neurotic, bodies gone mad. Not fulfilled, not at home.

If love happens, fear will disappear from the mind. You will have a life of freedom, at ease, at-homeness. No fear will come, no nightmares.

If prayer happens, then fear completely disappears, because with prayer you become one—you start feeling a deep relationship with the whole. From the spirit, fear disappears; the fear of death disappears when you pray, never before it.

And when you meditate, even fearlessness disappears. Fear disappears, fearlessness disappears. Nothing remains. Or, *only* the nothing remains. A vast purity, virginity, innocence.

## NOT A RELATIONSHIP, BUT A STATE OF BEING

Love is not a relationship. Love is a state of being; it has nothing to do with anybody else. One is not *in* love, one *is* love. And of course when one is love, one is in love—but that is an outcome, a by-product, that is not the source. The source is that one *is* love.

And who can be love? Certainly, if you are not aware of who you are, you cannot be love. You will be fear. Fear is just the opposite of love. Remember, hate is not the opposite of love, as people think. Hate is love standing upside down, it is not the opposite of love. The real opposite of love is fear. In love one expands, in fear one shrinks. In fear one becomes closed, in love one opens. In fear one doubts, in love one trusts. In fear one is left lonely. In love one disappears; hence there is no question of loneliness at all.

When one is not, how can one be lonely? Then these trees and the birds and the clouds and the sun and the stars are all within you. Love is when you have known your inner sky.

The young child is free of fear; children are born without any fear. If the society can help and support them to remain without fear, can help them to climb the trees and the mountains and swim the oceans and the rivers—if the society can help them in every possible way to become adventurers, adventurers of the unknown, and if the society can create a great inquiry instead of giving them dead beliefs— then the children will turn into great lovers, lovers of life. And that is true religion. There is no higher religion than love.

Meditate, dance, sing, and go deeper and deeper into yourself. Listen to the birds more attentively. Look at the flowers with awe, wonder. Don't become knowledgeable, don't go on labeling things. That's what knowledgeability is—the great art of labeling everything, categorizing everything. Meet people, mix with people, with as many people as possible, because each person expresses a different facet of God. Learn from people. Don't be afraid, this existence is not your enemy. This existence mothers you, this existence is ready to support you in every possible way. Trust, and you will start feeling a new upsurge of energy in you. That energy is love. That energy wants to bless the whole existence,

> The real opposite of love is fear.
> In love one expands, in fear one shrinks.
> In fear one becomes closed, in love one opens.
> In fear one doubts, in love one trusts.

because in that energy one feels blessed. And when you feel blessed, what else can you do except bless the whole existence?

Love is a deep desire to bless the whole existence.

## THIS CAKE IS DELICIOUS!

Love is very rare. To meet a person at his center is to pass through a revolution, because if you want to meet a person at his center you will have to allow that person to reach to your center also. You will have to become vulnerable, absolutely vulnerable, open.

It is risky. To allow somebody to reach your center is risky, dangerous, because you never know what that person will do to you. And once all your secrets are known, once your hiddenness has become unhidden, once you are exposed completely, what that other person will do you never know. The fear is there. That's why we never open.

With just an acquaintance, we think love has happened. Peripheries meet, and we think we have met. You are not your periphery. Really, the periphery is the boundary where you end, just the fencing around you. It is not you! The periphery is the place where you end and the world begins.

Even husbands and wives who have lived together for many years may be just acquaintances. They may not have known each other. And the more you live with someone the more you forget completely that the centers have remained unknown.

So the first thing to be understood is, don't take acquaintance as love. You may be making love, you may be sexually related, but sex is also peripheral. Unless centers meet, sex is just a meeting of two bodies. And a meeting of two bodies is not your meeting. Sex also remains acquaintance—physical, bodily, but still just an acquaintance. You can allow somebody to enter to your center only when you are not afraid, when you are not fearful.

There are two types of living: one fear-oriented, one love-oriented. Fear-oriented living can never lead you into deep relationship. You remain afraid, and the other cannot be allowed, cannot be allowed to penetrate you to your very core. To an extent you allow the other, but then the wall comes up and everything stops.

The love-oriented person is one who is not afraid of the future, one who is not afraid of the result and the consequence, who lives here and now. Don't be bothered about the result; that is the fear-oriented mind. Don't think about what will happen out of it. Just be here and act totally. Don't calculate. A fear-oriented man is always calculating, planning, arranging, safeguarding. His whole life is lost in this way.

I have heard about an old Zen monk:

He was on his deathbed. The last day had come, and he declared that on that evening he would be no more. So followers, disciples, friends started coming. He had many lovers, they all started coming; from far and wide people gathered.

One of his old disciples, when he heard that the Master was going to die, ran to the market. Somebody asked, "The Master is dying in his hut, why are you going to the market?" The old disciple said, "I know that my Master loves a particular type of cake, so I am going to purchase the cake."

It was difficult to find the cake, but by the evening somehow he managed. He came running with the cake.

And everybody was worried—it was as if the Master was waiting for someone. He would open his eyes and look, and close his eyes again. When this disciple came, he said, "Okay, so you have come. Where is the cake?" The disciple produced the cake—and he was very happy that the Master asked about it.

Dying, the Master took the cake in his hand . . . but his hand was not trembling. He was very old, but his hand was not trembling. So somebody asked, "You are so old and just on the verge of dying. The last breath is soon to leave you, but your hand is not trembling."

The Master said, "I never tremble, because there is no fear. My body has become old, but I am still young, and I will remain young even when the body is gone."

Then he took a bite, started munching the cake. And then somebody asked, "What is your last message, Master? You will be leaving us soon. What do you want us to remember?"

The Master smiled and said, "Ah, this cake is delicious."

This is a man who lives in the here and now: *This cake is delicious*. Even death is irrelevant. The next moment is meaningless. *This* moment, this cake is delicious. If you can be in this moment, this present moment, this presentness, the plenitude, then only can you love.

Love is a rare flowering. It happens only sometimes. Millions and millions of people live in the false attitude that they are lovers. They believe that they love, but that is their belief only.

Love is a rare flowering. Sometimes it happens. It is rare because it can happen only when there is no fear, never before. That means love can happen only to a very deeply spiritual, religious person. Sex is possible for all. Acquaintance is possible for all. Not love.

When you are not afraid, then there is nothing to hide; then you can be open, then you can withdraw all boundaries. And then you can invite the other to penetrate you to the very core.

And remember, if you allow somebody to penetrate you deeply, the other will allow you to penetrate into himself or herself, because when you allow somebody to penetrate you, trust is created. When you are not afraid, the other becomes fearless.

In your love, fear is always there. The husband is afraid of the wife, the wife is afraid of the husband. Lovers are always afraid. Then it is not love. Then it is just an arrangement of two fearful persons depending on each other, fighting, exploiting, manipulating, controlling, dominating, possessing—but it is not love.

> Love is a rare flowering. Sometimes it happens. It is rare because it can happen only when there is no fear, never before.

If you can allow love to happen, there is no need for prayer, there is no need for meditation, there is no need for any church, any temple. You can completely forget God if you can love—because through love, everything will have happened to you: meditation, prayer, God, *everything* will have happened to you. That's what Jesus means when he says love is God.

But love is difficult. Fear has to be dropped. And this is the strange thing, that you are so afraid and you have nothing to lose.

The mystic Kabir has said somewhere, "I look into people . . . they are so much afraid, but I can't see why—because they have nothing to lose." Says Kabir, "They are like a person who is naked but never goes to take a bath in the river because he is afraid—

where will he dry his clothes?" This is the situation you are in—naked, with no clothes, but always worried about the clothes.

What have you got to lose? Nothing. This body will be taken by death; before it is taken by death, give it to love. Whatsoever you have will be taken away; before it is taken away, why not share it? That is the *only* way of possessing it. If you can share and give, you are the master. It is going to be taken away—there is nothing you can retain forever. Death will destroy everything.

> This body will be taken by death, before it is taken by death, give it to love. Whatsoever you have will be taken away, before it is taken away, why not share it?

So, if you follow me rightly, the struggle is between death and love. If you can give, there will be no death. Before anything can be taken away from you, you will have already given it, you will have made it a gift. There can be no death.

For a lover there is no death. For a nonlover, every moment is a death because every moment something is being snatched away from him. The body is disappearing, he is losing every moment. And then there will be death, and everything will be annihilated.

What is the fear? Why are you so afraid? Even if everything is known about you and you are an open book, why fear? How can it harm you? Just false conceptions, just conditionings given by the society—that you have to hide, that you have to protect yourself, that you have to be constantly in a fighting mood, that everybody is an enemy, that everybody is against you.

Nobody is against you! Even if you feel somebody is against you, he too is not against you—because everybody is concerned with himself, not with you. There is nothing to fear. This has to be realized before a real relationship can happen. There is nothing to fear.

Meditate on it. And then allow the other to enter you, invite the other to enter you. Don't create any barrier anywhere; become a passage always open, no locks, no doors on you, no closed doors on you. Then love is possible.

When two centers meet, there is love. And love is an alchemical phenomenon—just like hydrogen and oxygen meet and a new thing, water, is created. You can have hydrogen, you can have oxygen, but if you are thirsty they will be useless. You can have as much oxygen as you want, as much hydrogen as you like, but the thirst will not go.

When two centers meet, a new thing is created. That new thing is love. And it is just like water; the thirst of many, many lives is satisfied. Suddenly you become content. That is the visible sign of love; you become content, as if you have achieved everything. There is nothing to achieve now; you have reached the goal. There is no further goal, destiny is fulfilled.

> Even if you feel somebody is against you, he too is not against you—because everybody is concerned with himself, not with you. There is nothing to fear. This has to be realized before a real relationship can happen.

The seed has become a flower, has come to its total flowering.

Deep contentment is the visible sign of love. Whenever a person is in love, he is in deep contentment. Love cannot be seen, but contentment, the deep satisfaction around him . . . his every breath, his every movement, his very being, content.

You may be surprised when I say to you that love makes you desireless, but desire comes with discontent. You desire because you don't have. You desire because you think that if you have something it will give you contentment. Desire comes out of discontent.

When there is love and two centers have met and dissolved and merged, and a new alchemical quality is born, contentment is there. It is as if the whole existence has stopped—no movement. Then the present moment is the only moment. And then you can say, "Ah, this cake is delicious." Even death doesn't mean anything to a man who is in love.

## A WORLD OF NO BOUNDARIES

Love is an opening into a world of no boundaries, into a world that ends nowhere. Love begins but ends never; it has a beginning but no end.

Remember one thing: ordinarily the mind interferes and does not allow love its infinity and its space. If you really love a person, you give him infinite space. Your very being is just a space for him to grow in, to grow with. The mind interferes and tries to possess the person, then love is destroyed. The mind is very greedy—the mind is greed. The mind is very poisonous. So if one wants to move into the world of love, one has to drop the mind. One has to live without the interference of the mind. The mind is good in its own place. It is needed in the market; it is not needed in love. It is needed when you are preparing a budget, but it is not needed when you are moving into inner space. It is needed when there is mathematics; it is not needed when there is meditation. So the mind has utility, but the utility is for the outside world. For the inner it is simply irrelevant. So become more and more loving . . . unconditionally loving. Become love. Become an opening—just be loving.

Birds and trees, earth and stars, men and women—everybody understands it. Black and white, there is only one language that is the language of the universe—that language is love. So become that language. And once you become love, a totally new world will open for you with no boundaries.

Always remember that the mind is the cause of helping people to become closed. The mind is very afraid of opening because the mind exists basically out of fear. The more fearless a person is, the less mind he uses. The more fearful a person, the more he uses the mind.

> If you really love a person, you give him infinite space.
> Your very being is just a space for him to grow in, to grow with.
> The mind interferes and tries to possess the person, then love is destroyed.

You may have observed that when you are afraid, when there is anxiety, when there is something that troubles you, the mind comes into focus very much. When you are anxious, the mind is there too much. When you are not anxious, the mind is not so much.

When everything is going well and there is no fear, the mind lags behind. When things go wrong, the mind simply jumps ahead of you, it becomes the leader. In times of danger it becomes the leader. The mind is just like the politicians. Adolf Hitler has written in his autobiography, *Mein Kampf,* that you should always keep the country in fear if you want to remain in the leadership. Keep the country always afraid that the neighbor is going to attack, that there are countries who are designing an attack, that they are preparing to attack—go on creating rumors. Never leave people at ease, because when they are at ease they don't bother about the politicians. When people are really at ease, politicians are meaningless. Keep people always afraid, then the politician is powerful.

> The more fearless a person is, the less mind he uses. The more fearful a person, the more he uses the mind.

Whenever there is war the politician becomes a great man. Churchill or Hitler or Stalin or Mao—they are all products of war. If there were no Second World War there would be no Winston Churchill and no Hitler and no Stalin. War creates situations, gives opportunities for people to dominate and become leaders. Exactly the same is the politics of the mind.

Meditation is nothing but creating a situation where the mind has less and less things to do. You are so unafraid, you are so loving, you are so peaceful—you are so contented with whatsoever is happening that the mind has nothing to say. Then the mind by and by lags behind, lags behind, and more and more distance is created.

One day the mind completely recedes—then you become a universe. Then you are no more confined to your body, no more confined by anything—you are pure space. That's what God is. God is pure space.

Love is the way toward that pure space. Love is the means and God is the end.

PEOPLE WHO ARE AFRAID ARE THE PEOPLE WHO ARE CAPABLE OF TREMENDOUS LOVE. Fear is a negative aspect of love. If love is not allowed to flow, it becomes fear. If love is allowed to flow, fear disappears. That's why only in moments of love there is no fear. If you love a person, suddenly fear disappears.

> Meditation is nothing but creating a situation where the mind has less and less things to do.

Lovers are the only people who are fearless; even death creates no problem. Only lovers can die in tremendous silence and fearlessness.

But it always happens that the more you love, the more you feel fear. That's why women feel more fear than men, because they have more potentiality for love. In this world there are very few possibilities to actualize your love, so it remains hanging around you. And if any potentiality remains hanging, it turns to its opposite. It can become jealousy; that too is part of fear. It can become possessiveness; that too is part of fear. It can become even hatred; that too is part of fear. So be more and more loving. Love uncondi-tionally, and love in as many ways as possible. One can love in millions of ways.

One can just love a stranger passing on the road. One can just feel love for him, and go on one's way. There is no need to even talk. There is no need to communicate it. One can simply feel and go on one's own way. One can love a rock. One can love the trees, one can love the sky, the stars. One can love the friend, the husband, the children, the father, the mother. One can love in millions of ways.

> If love is not allowed to flow, it becomes fear. If love is allowed to flow, fear disappears.

REMEMBER: BRAVE DOES NOT MEAN FEARLESS. If somebody is fearless you cannot call him brave. You cannot call a machine brave; it is fearless. Bravery exists only in the ocean of fear, bravery is an island in the ocean of fear. Fear is there, but in spite of the fear one takes the risk— that is bravery. One trembles, one is afraid to go into the dark, and still one goes. In spite of oneself one goes; that is the meaning of being brave. It does not mean fearless. It means full of fear but still not being dominated by it.

The greatest question arises when you move into love. Then fear grips your soul, because to love means to die, to die into the other. It is death, and a far deeper death than ordinary death. In the ordinary death only the body dies; in the death of love the ego dies. To love needs great guts. It needs one to be capable of going into it in spite of all the fears that will clamor around one.

The greater the risk, the greater the possibility of growth—so nothing helps a man more in growth than love. People who are afraid of being in love remain childish, remain immature, unripe. It is only the fire of love that gives you ripeness.

## NEITHER EASY NOR DIFFICULT, JUST NATURAL

Love is a natural state of consciousness. It is neither easy nor difficult, those words don't apply to it at all. It is not an effort; hence, it can't be easy and it can't be difficult either. It is like breathing! It is like your heartbeat, it is like blood circulating in your body.

Love is your very being . . . but that love has become almost impossible. The society does not allow it. The society conditions you in such a way that love becomes impossible and hate becomes the only possible thing. Then hate is easy, and love is not only difficult but impossible. Man has been distorted. Man cannot be reduced to slavery if he is not distorted first. The politician and the priest have been in a deep conspiracy down the ages. They have been reducing humanity to a crowd of slaves. They are destroying every possibility of rebellion in man—and love is rebellion, because love listens only to the heart and does not care a bit about anything else.

Love is dangerous because it makes you an individual. And the state and the church . . . they don't want individuals, not at all. They don't want human beings, they want sheep. They want people who only look like human beings but whose souls have been crushed so utterly, damaged so deeply, that it seems almost irreparable.

And the best way to destroy man is to destroy his spontaneity of love. If man has love, there can't be nations; nations exist on hate. The Indians hate the Pakistanis, and the Pakistanis hate the Indians— only then can these two countries exist. If love appears, boundaries will disappear. If love appears, then who will be a Christian and then who will be a Jew? If love appears, religions will disappear.

> If your life is a dance, God has been attained already. The loving heart is full of God. There is no need for any search, there is no need for any prayer, there is no need to go to any temple, to any priest.

If love appears, who is going to go to the temple? For what? It is because love is missing that you are searching for God. God is nothing but a substitute for your missing love. Because you are not blissful, because you are not peaceful, because you are not ecstatic, you are searching for God—otherwise, who bothers? Who cares? If your life is a dance, God has been attained already. The loving heart is full of God. There is no need for any search, there is no need for any prayer, there is no need to go to any temple, to any priest.

Hence the priest and the politician, these two, are the enemies of humanity. They are in a conspiracy, because the politician wants to rule your body and the priest wants to rule your soul. And the secret is the same: destroy love. Then a man is nothing but a hollowness, an emptiness, a meaningless existence. Then you can do whatsoever you want with humanity and nobody will rebel, nobody will have courage enough to rebel.

Love gives courage, love takes all fear away—and the oppressors depend on your fear. They create fear in you, a thousand and one kinds of fear. You are surrounded by fears, your whole psychology is full of fears. Deep down you are trembling. Only on the surface do you keep a certain facade; otherwise, inside there are layers and layers of fear.

A man full of fear can only hate—hate is a natural outcome of fear. A man full of fear is also full of anger, and a man full of fear is more against life than for life. Death seems to be a restful state to the fear-filled man. The fearful man is suicidal, he is life-negative. Life seems to be dangerous to him, because to live means you will have to love—how can you live? Just as the body needs breathing to live, the soul needs love to live. And love is utterly poisoned.

By poisoning your love energy they have created a split in you; they have made an enemy within you, they have divided you in two. They have created a civil war, and you are always in conflict. And in conflict your energy is dissipated; hence your life does not have zestfulness, cheerfulness. It is not overflowing with energy; it is dull, insipid, it is unintelligent.

Love sharpens intelligence, fear dulls it. Who wants you to be intelligent? Not those who are in power. How can they want you to be intelligent?—because if you are intelligent you will start seeing the whole strategy, their games. They want you to be stupid and mediocre. They certainly want you to be efficient as far as work is concerned, but not intelligent; hence humanity lives at the lowest, at the minimum of its potential.

Scientific researchers say that the ordinary man uses only five percent of his potential intelligence in his whole life. The ordinary man, only five percent—what about the extraordinary? What about an Albert Einstein, a Mozart, a Beethoven? The researchers say that even those who are very talented don't use more than ten percent. And those whom we call geniuses use only fifteen percent.

Think of a world where everybody is using one hundred percent of his potential . . . then the gods will be jealous of earth, then gods would like to be born on earth. Then the earth will be a paradise, a super-paradise. Right now it is a hell.

> Think of a world where everybody is using one hundred percent of his potential . . . then the gods will be jealous of earth, then gods would like to be born on earth. Then the earth will be a paradise.

If man is left alone, unpoisoned, then love will be simple, very simple. There will be no problem. It will be just like water flowing downward, or vapor rising upward, trees blossoming, birds singing. It will be so natural and so spontaneous!

But man is not left alone. As the child is born, the oppressors are ready to jump on him, to crush his energies, to distort them to such an extent, to distort them so deeply that the person will never become aware that he is living a false life, a pseudo life, that he is not living as he was meant to live, as he was born to live; that he is living something synthetic, plastic, that this is not his real soul. That's why millions of people are in such misery—because they feel somewhere that they have been distracted, that they are not their own selves, that something has gone basically wrong. . . .

Love is simple if the child is allowed to grow, helped to grow, in natural ways. If the child is helped to be in harmony with nature and in harmony with himself, if the child is in every way supported, nourished, encouraged to be natural and to be himself, a light unto himself, then love is simple. One will be simply loving!

Hate will be almost impossible because before you can hate somebody else, first you have to create the poison within yourself. You can give something to somebody only if you have it. You can hate only if you are full of hate. And to be full of hate is to suffer hell. To be full of hate is to be on fire. To be full of hate means you are wounding yourself first. Before you can wound somebody else, you have to wound yourself. The other may not be wounded, it will depend on the other. But one thing is absolutely certain: that before you can hate, you have to go through long suffering and misery. The other may not accept your hatred, may reject it. The other may be a buddha—he may simply laugh at it. He may forgive you, he may not react. You may not be able to wound him if he is not ready to react. If you cannot disturb him, what can you do? You will feel impotent before him.

> If you hate somebody, first you have to wound your own soul in so many ways, you have to be so full of poison that you can throw poison on others.

So it is not necessarily so that the other is going to be wounded. But one thing is absolutely certain, that if you hate somebody, first you have to wound your own soul in so many ways; you have to be so full of poison that you can throw poison on others.

Hate is unnatural. Love is a state of health; hate is a state of illness. Just like illness it is unnatural. It happens only when you lose track of nature, when you are no longer in harmony with existence, no longer in harmony with your being, with your innermost core. Then you are ill—psychologically, spiritually ill. Hatred is only a symbol of illness, and love one of health and wholeness and holiness.

Love should be one of the most natural things, but it is not. On the contrary, it has become the most difficult thing—almost the impossible thing. Hate has become easy; you are trained, you are prepared for hate. To be a Hindu is to be full of hate for Mohammedans, for Christians, for Jews; to be a Christian is to be full of hate for other religions. To be a nationalist is to be full of hate for other nations.

You know only one way of love, that is to hate others. You can show your love for your country only by hating other countries, and you can show your love for your church only by hating other churches. You are in a mess!

These so-called religions go on talking about love, and all that they do in the world is create more and more hate. Christians talk about love and they have been creating wars, crusades. Mohammedans talk about love and they have been creating jihads, religious wars. Hindus talk about love, but you can look into their scriptures—they are full of hate, hate for other religions. And we accept all this nonsense! And we accept it without any resistance because we have been conditioned to accept these things, we have been taught that this is how things are. And then you go on denying your own nature.

Love has been poisoned but not destroyed. The poison can be thrown out, out of your system—you can be cleansed. You can vomit all that the society has enforced upon you. You can drop all your beliefs and all your conditionings—you can be free. The society cannot keep you a slave forever if you decide to be free.

It is time to drop out of all old patterns and start a new way of life, a natural way of life, a nonrepressive way of life, a life not of renunciation but of rejoicing. Hate will become more and more impossible. Hate is the polar opposite of love, in the sense that illness is the polar opposite of health. But you need not choose illness.

Illness has a few advantages that health cannot have; don't become attached to those advantages. Hate also has a few advantages that love cannot have. And you have to be very watchful. The ill person gets sympathy from everybody else; nobody hurts him, everybody remains careful what they say to him, he is so ill. He remains the focus, the center of everybody—the family, the friends— he becomes the central person, he becomes important. Now, if he becomes too much attached to this importance, to this ego fulfillment, he will never want to be healthy again. He himself will cling to illness. And psychologists say there are many people who are clinging to illnesses because of the advantages illnesses have. And they have invested in their illnesses for so long that they have completely forgotten that they are clinging

> Love should be one of the most natural things, but it is not. On the contrary, it has become the most difficult thing—almost the impossible thing. Hate has become easy; you are trained, you are prepared for hate.

to those illnesses. They are afraid if they become healthy they will be nobody again.

You teach that, too. When a small child becomes ill, the whole family is so attentive. This is absolutely unscientific. When the child is ill, take care of his body but don't pay too much attention. It is dangerous, because if illness and your attention become associated . . . which is bound to happen if it is repeated again and again.

> It is time to drop out of all old patterns and start a new way of life, a natural way of life, a nonrepressive way of life, a life not of renunciation but of rejoicing.

Whenever the child is ill he becomes the center of the whole family: daddy comes and sits by his side and inquires about his health, and the doctor comes, and the neighbors start coming, and friends inquire, and people bring presents for him. . . . Now he can become too much attached to all this; it can be so nourishing to his ego that he may not like to be well again. And if this happens, then it is impossible to be healthy. No medicine can help now. The person has become decisively committed to illness. And that's what has happened to many people, the majority.

When you hate, your ego is fulfilled. The ego can exist only if it hates, because in hating you feel superior, in hating you become separate, in hating you become defined. In hating you attain a certain identity. In love the ego has to disappear. In love you are no longer separate—love helps you to dissolve with others. It is a meeting and a merger.

If you are too much attached to the ego, then hate is easy and love is most difficult. Be alert, watchful: hate is the shadow of ego. Love needs great courage. It needs great courage because it needs the sacrifice of the ego. Only those who are ready to become no-bodies are able to love. Only those who are ready to become nothing, utterly empty of themselves, are able to receive the gift of love from the beyond.

# TAKE YOURSELF OUT OF THE CROWD

*Meditation is just a courage to be silent and alone.*

*Slowly slowly, you start feeling a new quality to yourself, a new aliveness, a new beauty, a new intelligence—which is not borrowed from anybody, which is growing within you. It has roots in your existence. And if you are not a coward, it will come to fruition, to flowering.*

Nobody is what he was meant by existence to be. The society, the culture, the religion, the education have all been conspiring against innocent children. They have all the powers—the child is helpless and dependent, so whatsoever they want to make out of him, they manage to do it. They don't allow any child to grow to his natural destiny. Their every effort is to make human beings into utilities. Who knows, if a child is left on his own to grow, whether he will be of any use to the vested interests or not? The society is not prepared to take the risk. It grabs the child and starts molding him into something that is needed by the society.

In a certain sense, it kills the soul of the child and gives him a false identity so that he never misses his soul, his being. The false identity is a substitute. But that substitute is useful only in the same crowd which has given it to you. The moment you are alone, the false starts falling apart and the repressed real starts expressing itself. Hence the fear of being lonely.

Nobody wants to be lonely. Everybody wants to belong to a crowd—not only one crowd, but many crowds. A person belongs to a religious crowd, a political party, a Rotary Club . . . and there are many other small groups to belong to. One wants to be supported twenty-four hours a day because the false, without support, cannot stand. The moment one is alone, one starts feeling a strange craziness. For so many years you believed yourself to be somebody, and then suddenly in a moment of loneliness you start feeling you are not that. It creates fear: then who are you?

And years of suppression . . . it will take some time for the real to express itself. The gap between the two has been called by the mystics "the dark night of the soul"—a very appropriate expression. You are no more the false, and you are not yet the real. You are in a limbo, you don't know who you are.

Particularly in the West, the problem is even more complicated because they have not developed any methodology to discover the real as soon as possible, so that the dark night of the soul can be shortened. The West knows nothing as far as meditation is concerned. And meditation is only a name for being alone, silent, waiting for the real to assert itself. It is not an act, it is a silent relaxation—because whatever you "do" will come out of your false personality . . . all your doing, for so many years, has come out of it. It is an old habit.

Habits die hard. So many years of living in a false personality imposed by people whom you loved, whom you respected . . . and they were not intentionally doing anything bad to you. Their intentions were good, just their awareness was nil. They were not conscious people—your parents, your teachers, your priests, your politicians—they were not conscious people, they were unconscious. And even a good intention in the hands of an unconscious person turns out to be poisonous.

So whenever you are alone, a deep fear—because suddenly the false starts disappearing. And the real will take a little time, you have lost it so many years ago. You will have to give some consideration to the fact that so many years' gap has to be bridged.

In fear—that "I am losing myself, my senses, my sanity, my mind, everything" . . . because the self that has been given to you by others consists of all these things—it looks like you will go insane. You immediately start doing something just to keep yourself engaged. If there are no people, at least there is some action, so the false remains engaged and does not start disappearing.

Hence people find it the most difficult on holidays. For five days they work, hoping that on the weekend they are going to relax. But the weekend is the worst time in the whole world—more accidents happen on the weekend, more people commit suicide, more murders, more stealing, more rape. Strange . . . and these people were engaged for five days and there was no problem. But the weekend suddenly gives them a choice, either to be engaged in something or to relax—but relaxing is fearsome; the false personality disappears. Keep engaged, do anything stupid. People are running toward the beaches, bumper to bumper, miles-long traffic. And if you ask them where they are going, they are "getting away from the crowd"—and the whole crowd is going with them! They are going to find a solitary, silent space—all of them.

In fact, if they had remained home it would have been more solitary and silent—because all the idiots have gone in search of a solitary place. And they are rushing like mad, because two days will be finished soon, they have to reach—don't ask where!

On the beaches, you see . . . they are so crowded, not even marketplaces are so crowded. And strangely enough, people are feeling very much at ease, taking a sunbath. Ten thousand people on a small beach taking a sunbath, relaxing. The same person on the same beach alone will not be able to relax. But he knows thousands of other people are relaxing all around him. The same people were in the offices, the same people were in the streets, the same people were in the marketplace, now the same people are on the beach.

The crowd is an essential for the false self to exist. The moment it is lonely, you start freaking out. This is where one should understand a little bit of meditation.

Don't be worried, because that which can disappear is worth disappearing. It is meaningless to cling to it—it is not yours, it is not you.

You are the one when the false has gone and the fresh, the innocent, the unpolluted being will arise in its place. Nobody else can answer your question "Who am I?"—you will know it.

All meditative techniques are a help to destroy the false. They don't give you the real—the real cannot be given.

That which can be given cannot be real. The real you have got already; just the false has to be taken away.

In a different way it can be said: a Master takes away things from you which you don't really have, and he gives you that which you really have.

Meditation is just a courage to be silent and alone. Slowly slowly, you start feeling a new quality to yourself, a new aliveness, a new beauty, a new intelligence—which is not borrowed from anybody, which is growing within you. It has roots in your existence. And if you are not a coward, it will come to fruition, to flowering.

Only the brave, the courageous, the people who have guts, can be religious. Not the churchgoers—these are the cowards. Not the Hindus, not the Mohammedans, not the Christians—they are against searching. The same crowd, they are trying to make their false identity more consolidated.

You were born, you have come into the world with life, with consciousness, with tremendous sensitivity. Just look at a small child—look at his eyes, the freshness. All that has been covered by a false personality.

> ⟡
>
> All meditative techniques are a help to destroy the false. They don't give you the real—the real cannot be given. That which can be given cannot be real. The real you have got already, just the false has to be taken away.

There is no need to be afraid. You can lose only that which has to be lost. And it is good to lose it soon—because the longer it stays, the stronger it becomes.

And one does not know anything about tomorrow.

Don't die before realizing your authentic being.

Only those few people are fortunate who have lived with authentic being and who have died with authentic being—because they know that life is eternal, and death is a fiction.

## THE POLITICS OF NUMBERS

In a society, there is a deep expectation that you will behave exactly like others. The moment you behave a little bit differently you become a stranger, and people are very much afraid of strangers.

That's why everywhere if two persons are sitting in the bus, in a railway train, or just at a bus stop, they cannot sit silently—because silently they are both strangers. They immediately start introducing each other—"Who are you? Where are you going? What do you do, your business?" A few things . . . and they settle down; you are another human being just like them.

People continuously want to be in a crowd in which they fit. The moment you behave differently, the whole crowd becomes suspicious; something is going wrong. They know you, and they can see the change. They have known you when you never accepted yourself, and now they suddenly see that you accept yourself . . .

In this society nobody accepts himself. Everybody is condemning himself. This is the lifestyle of the society: condemn yourself. And if you are not condemning yourself, if you are accepting yourself, you have fallen away from the society. And the society does not tolerate anybody who falls out of the fold because the society lives by numbers; it is a politics of numbers. When there are many numbers, people feel good. Vast numbers make people feel that they must be right—they cannot be wrong, millions of people are with them. And when they are left alone great doubts start arising: Nobody is with me. What is the guarantee that I am right?

That's why I say that in this world, to be an individual is the greatest courage.

The most fearless grounding is needed to be an individual: "It does not matter that the whole world is against me. What matters is that my experience is valid. I don't look at the numbers, at how many people are with me. I look at the validity of my experience—at whether I am just repeating somebody else's words like a parrot, or the source of my statements is in my own experience. If it is in my own experience, if it is part of my blood and bones and marrow, then the whole world can be on one side; still, I am right and they are wrong. It doesn't matter, I don't need their votes for me in order to feel right. Only people who carry the opinions of others need the support of others."

But that's how human society has functioned up to now. That's

> The society lives by numbers; it is a politics of numbers. When there are many numbers, people feel good. Vast numbers make people feel that they must be right—they cannot be wrong, millions of people are with them.

how they keep you within the fold. If they are sad, you have to be sad; if they are miserable, you have to be miserable. Whatever they are, you have to be the same. Difference is not allowed because difference ultimately leads to individuals, uniqueness, and society is very much afraid of individuals and uniqueness. That means somebody has become independent of the crowd, he does not care a bit about the crowd. Your gods, your temples, your priests, your scriptures, all have become meaningless for him.

Now he has his own being and his own way, his own style—to live, to die, to celebrate, to sing, to dance. He has come home.

And nobody can come home with a crowd. Everybody can come home only alone.

## LISTEN TO YOUR "INNER SENSE"

A boy was constantly scratching his head. His father looked at him one day and said, "Son, why are you always scratching your head?"

"Well," the boy responded, "I guess because I am the only one who knows it itches."

This is inner sense! Only you know. Nobody else can know. It cannot be observed from the outside. When you have a headache, only you know—you cannot prove it. When you are happy, only you know—you cannot prove it. You cannot put it on the table to be inspected by everybody, dissected, analyzed.

In fact, the inner sense is so inner that you cannot even prove that it exists. That's why science goes on denying it, but the denial is inhuman. Even the scientist knows that when he feels love, he has an inner feeling. Something *is* there! It is not a thing, and it is not an object, and it is not possible to put it before others—and still it *is*.

Inner sense has its own validity. But because of the scientific training, people have lost trust in their inner sense. They depend on others. You depend so much that if somebody says, "You are looking very happy," you start feeling happy. If twenty people decide to make you unhappy, they can make you unhappy. They just have to repeat it the whole day—whenever you come across them, they have to say to you, "You are looking very unhappy, very sad. What is the matter? Somebody died or something?" And you will start suspecting: so many people are saying that you are unhappy, you must be.

> ☞
>
> The most fearless grounding is needed to be an individual: "It does not matter that the whole world is against me. What matters is that my experience is valid."

You depend on people's opinions. You have depended on people's opinions so much that you have lost all track of inner sense. This inner sense has to be rediscovered, because all that is beautiful and all that is good and all that is divine can be felt only by the inner sense.

Stop being influenced by people's opinions. Rather, start looking in . . . allow your inner sense to say things to you. Trust it. If you trust it, it will grow. If you trust it, you will feed it, it will become stronger.

Vivekananda went to Ramakrishna, and he said, "There is no God! I can prove it—there is no God." He was a very logical, skeptical man, well educated in Western philosophical thinking. Ramakrishna was an uneducated, illiterate person. And Ramakrishna says, "Okay, so prove!"

Vivekananda talked much, gave all the proofs that he had. And Ramakrishna listened, and then he said, "But my inner sense says God is—and that is the final authority. All that you are saying is argumentation. What does your inner sense say?"

Vivekananda had not even thought about it. He shrugged his shoulders. He had read books, he had collected arguments, proofs for and against, and he had tried to decide whether God exists or not according to these proofs. But he had not looked in. He had not asked his inner sense.

It is so stupid, but the skeptical mind *is* stupid, the logical mind is stupid.

Ramakrishna said, "Your arguments are beautiful, I enjoyed. But what can I do? I *know!* My inner sense says he is. Just as my inner sense says I am happy, I am ill, I am sad, my stomach is hurting, that today I am not feeling well, so my inner sense says God is. It is not a question of debate."

And Ramakrishna said, "I cannot prove it, but if you want, I can show you." Nobody had told Vivekananda before that God can be shown. And before he could say anything Ramakrishna jumped—he was a wild man—he jumped and put his feet on Vivekananda's chest! And something happened, some energy jumped, and Vivekananda fell into a trance for three hours. When he opened his eyes, he was a totally different man.

Ramakrishna said, "What do you say now? God is, or God is not? What does your inner sense say now?"

He was in such tranquillity, such stillness, as he had never known before. There was such jubilation inside, such well-being, such overflowing well-being. . . . He had to bow down and touch Ramakrishna's feet and say, "Yes, God is."

God is not a person but the ultimate sense of well-being, the ultimate sense of being at home, the ultimate sense that "I belong to this world and this world belongs to me. I am not alien here, I am not an outsider." The ultimate sense—existential—that, "This whole and I are not separate." This experience is God. But this experience is possible only if you allow your inner sense to function.

Start allowing it! Give it as many opportunities as possible. Don't look always for outside authorities, and don't look for outside opinions. Keep yourself a little more independent. Feel more, think less.

Go and look at the rose flower, and don't just repeat parrotlike, "This is beautiful." This may be just opinion, people have told you; from your very childhood you have been hearing, "The rose flower is beautiful, is a great flower." So when you see the rose, you simply repeat like a computer, "This is beautiful." Are you really feeling it? Is it your inner feeling? If it is not, don't say it.

Looking at the moon, don't say that it is beautiful—unless it is your inner sense. You will be surprised that ninety-nine percent of the stuff that you carry in your mind is all borrowed. And within that ninety-nine percent of stuff, useless rubbish, the one percent of inner sense is lost, is drowned. Drop that knowledgeability. Recover your inner sense.

It is through the inner sense that God is known.

There are six senses: five are outer; they tell you about the world. Eyes say something about the light; without eyes you will not know light. Ears say something about the sound; without ears you will not know anything about sound. There is a sixth sense, the inner sense, that shows and tells you something about yourself and the ultimate source of things. That sense has to be discovered.

Meditation is nothing but the discovery of the inner sense.

**THE GREATEST FEAR IN THE WORLD IS OF THE OPINIONS OF OTHERS.** And the moment you are unafraid of the crowd you are no longer a sheep, you become a lion. A great roar arises in your heart, the roar of freedom.

Buddha has actually called it the lion's roar. When a man reaches an absolutely silent state he roars like a lion. For the first time he knows what freedom is because now there is no fear of anybody's opinion. What people say does not matter. Whether they call you a saint or a sinner is immaterial;

God is not a person but the ultimate sense of well-being, the ultimate sense of being at home, the ultimate sense that "I belong to this world and this world belongs to me. I am not alien here, I am not an outsider."

your whole and sole judge is God. And by God a person is not meant at all; God simply means the whole universe.

It is not a question of having to face a person; you have to face the trees, the rivers, the mountains, the stars—the whole universe. And this is our universe, we are part of it. There is no need to be afraid of it, there is no need to hide anything from it. In fact even if you try you cannot hide. The whole knows it already, the whole knows more about you than you know.

> *This is our universe, we are part of it. There is no need to be afraid of it, there is no need to hide anything from it. In fact even if you try you cannot hide. The whole knows it already, the whole knows more about you than you know.*

And the second point is even more significant: God has already judged. It is not something that is going to happen in the future, it has already happened: he has judged. So even the fear of that judgment withers away. It is not a question of some Judgment Day at the end. You need not tremble. The judgment day happened on the first day; the moment he created you he already judged you. He knows you, you are his creation. If something goes wrong with you he is responsible, not you. If you go astray he is responsible, not you. How can you be responsible?—you are not your own creation. If you paint and something goes wrong you cannot say that the painting is the cause of it—the painter is the cause.

So there is no need to be afraid of the crowd or of some imaginary God at the end of the world asking you what you have done and what you have not done. He has already judged—that is really significant—it has already happened, so you are free. And the moment one knows that one is totally free to be oneself, life starts having a dynamic quality to it.

Fear creates fetters, freedom gives you wings.

## FREEDOM FROM, FREEDOM FOR

Never think in terms of being free *from;* always think in terms of being free *for.* And the difference is vast, tremendously vast. Don't think in terms of from—think for. Be free for God, be free for truth, but don't think that you want to be free from the crowd, free from the church, free from this and that. You may be able to go far away one day, but you will never be free, never. It is going to be some sort of suppression.

Why are you so afraid of the crowd? . . . If the pull is there, then your fear simply shows your pull, your attraction. Wherever you go you will remain dominated by the crowd.

What I am saying is just look at the facts of it—that there is no need to think in terms of the crowd. Just think in terms of your being. It can be dropped right now. You cannot be free if you struggle. You can drop it because there is no point in struggling.

The crowd is not the problem—you are the problem. The crowd is not pulling you—you are being pulled, not by somebody else but by your own unconscious conditioning. Always remember not to throw the responsibility somewhere on somebody else, because then you will never be free of it. Deep down it is your responsibility. Why should one be so much against the crowd? Poor crowd! Why should you be so much against it? Why do you carry such a wound?

The crowd cannot do anything unless you cooperate. So the question is of your cooperation. You can drop the cooperation just now, just like that. If you put any effort into it, then you will be in trouble. So do it instantly. It is just on the spur of the moment, of spontaneous understanding, if you can see the point that if you fight, you will be fighting a losing battle. In the very fighting you are emphasizing the crowd.

> The crowd is not pulling you—you are being pulled, not by somebody else but by your own unconscious conditioning.

That's what has happened to millions of people. Somebody wants to escape from women—in India they have done that for centuries. Then they become more and more engrossed in it. They want to get rid of sex and their whole mind then becomes sexual; they think only of sex and nothing else. They fast, and they will not go to sleep; they will do this and that *pranayama* and yoga and a thousand and one things—all nonsense. The more they fight with sex the more they are enforcing it, the more they are concentrating on it. It becomes so significant, out of all proportion.

That is what has happened to Christian monasteries. They became so repressed, just afraid. The same can happen to you if you become afraid too much of the crowd. The crowd cannot do anything unless you cooperate, so it is a question of your alertness. Don't cooperate!

This is my observation: that whatsoever happens to you, you are responsible. Nobody else is doing it to you. You wanted it to be done, so it has been done. Somebody exploits you because you wanted to be exploited. Somebody has put you into a prison because you wanted to be imprisoned. There must have been a certain search for it. Maybe you used to call it security. Your names may have been different, your labels may have been different, but you were hankering to be imprisoned because in a prison one is safe and there is no insecurity.

But don't fight with the prison walls. Look inside. Find that hankering for security and how the crowd can manipulate you. You must be asking for something from the crowd—recognition, honor, respect, respectability. If you ask them, you have to repay them. Then the crowd says, "Okay, we give you respect, and you give us your freedom." It is a simple bargain. But the crowd has never done anything to you—it is basically you. So get out of your own way!

## FIND YOUR ORIGINAL FACE

Just be what you are and don't care a bit about the world. Then you will feel a tremendous relaxation and a deep peace within your heart. This is what Zen people call your "original face"—relaxed, without tensions, without pretensions, without hypocrisies, without the so-called disciplines of how you should behave.

And remember, the original face is a beautiful poetic expression, but it does not mean that you will have a different face. This same face will lose all its tensions, this same face will be relaxed, this same face will be nonjudgmental, this same face will not think of others as inferior. This same face under these new values will be your original face.

There is an ancient proverb: Many a hero is a man who did not have the courage to be a coward.

> This is my observation: that whatsoever happens to you, you are responsible. Nobody else is doing it to you. You wanted it to be done, so it has been done.

If you are a coward, what is wrong in it? You are a coward—it is perfectly good. Cowards are also needed, otherwise from where will you get heroes? They are an absolute necessity to give the background to create heroes.

Just be yourself, whatever it is.

The problem is that never before has anybody told you just to be yourself. Everybody is poking his nose in, saying that you should be this way, you should be that way—even in ordinary matters.

In my school . . . I was just a small boy, but I hated to be told how I have to be. Teachers started bribing me—"If you behave rightly, you can become a genius."

I said, "To hell with the genius—I simply want to be myself." I used to sit with my legs on the table, and every teacher was offended. They would say, "What kind of behavior is this?"

I said, "The table is not saying anything to me. It is something between me and the table, so why are you looking so angry? I am not putting my legs on your head! You should relax just as I am relaxing. And this way I feel better able to understand what nonsense you are teaching."

Just on one side of the room was a beautiful window, and outside were trees and birds and cuckoos. Mostly I was looking out of the window, and the teacher would come and say, "Why do you come to school at all?"

I said, "Because in my house there is no window like this, which opens up to the whole sky. And around my house there are no cuckoos, no birds. The house is in the city, surrounded by other houses, so crowded that birds don't come there, cuckoos don't feel that these are the people to be blessed by their songs.

> If you are a coward, what is wrong in it? You are a coward—it is perfectly good. Cowards are also needed, otherwise from where will you get heroes?

"Forget the idea that I come here to listen to you! I am paying my fee, you are simply a servant and you should remember that. If I fail I will not come to complain to you; if I fail I will not feel sad. But if for the whole year I have to pretend that I am listening to you, while I am listening to the cuckoos outside, that will be the beginning of a hypocritical life. And I don't want to be a hypocrite."

On every matter the teachers, the professors wanted you to do it in a certain way. In my school in those days, and perhaps even today, using a cap was necessary. I have nothing against caps; since

I have left the university I have started wearing caps, but I never wore one until I left the university. The first teacher who was worried about me said, "You are disturbing the discipline of the school. Where is your cap?"

I said, "Bring the school code of behavior. Is there any mention that every boy should wear a cap? And if there is not, you are imposing something against the school code."

He took me to the principal of the school, and I told the principal, "I am absolutely ready, just show me where it is written that a cap is compulsory. If it is compulsory I may even leave the school, but first let me see where it is written."

There was no written code, and I said, "Can you give me any other reasonable arguments for using the cap? Will it increase my intelligence? Will it increase my life? Will it give me better health, more understanding?" I said, "As far as I know, Bengal is the only province in India where caps are not used, and that is the most intelligent part of the country. Punjab is just the opposite. There, for a cap, people use turbans—such big turbans, as if their intelligence is escaping so they are trying to keep hold of it. And that is the most unintelligent part of the country."

The principal said, "There seems to be some sense in what you are saying, but it is a school discipline. If you stop wearing a cap, then others will stop."

I said, "Then what is the fear? Just drop the whole convention."

Nobody wants to allow you to be yourself on matters that are absolutely insignificant.

I used to have long hair in my childhood. And I used to come in and out of my father's shop, because the shop and the home were connected. The home was behind the shop and it was absolutely necessary to pass through the shop. People would ask, "Whose girl is this?"—because my hair was so long, they could not imagine that a boy would have such long hair.

My father felt very ashamed and embarrassed to say, "He is a boy."

"But," they said, "then why all this hair?"

One day—it was not his normal nature—he became so embarrassed and angry that he came and cut my hair with his own hands. Bringing the scissors that he used to cut cloth in his shop, he cut my hair. I didn't say anything to him—he was surprised. He said, "You don't have anything to say?"

I said, "I will say it in my own way."

"So what do you mean?"

I said, "You will see." And I went to the opium-addict barber who used to have a shop just in front of our house. He was the only man I had a respect for. There were a row of barbershops, but I loved that old man. He was a rare variety, and he loved me; for hours we used to talk to each other.

I went to him and I told him, "Just shave my whole head completely." In India the head is shaved completely only when your father dies. For a moment even that opium addict came to his senses. He said, "What has happened? Has your father died?"

I said, "Don't bother about these things. You do what I am saying; it is none of your concern! You just cut my hair completely, shave it completely."

So the barber said, "That's right. It is none of my concern. If he has died, he has died."

He shaved my head completely, and I went home. I passed through the shop. My father looked and all his customers looked.

They said, "What happened? Whose boy is this? His father has died."

My father said, "He is my boy and I am alive! But I knew he was going to do something. He has answered me well."

Wherever I went people would ask, "What happened? He was perfectly healthy."

I said, "People die at any age. You are worried about him, you are not worried about my hairs."

That was the last thing my father ever did to me, because he knew that the answer could be more dangerous! I said to him, "You created the whole mess. What was there to be embarrassed about? You could have said, 'She is my girl.' I don't have any objection about that. But you should not have interfered with me the way you did. It was violent, barbarous. Rather than saying anything to me, you simply started cutting my hair."

Nobody allows anybody to be just himself. And you have learned all those ideas so deeply that it seems they are your ideas. Just relax. Forget all those conditionings, drop them like dry leaves falling from the trees. It is better to be a naked tree without any leaves than to have plastic leaves and plastic foliage and plastic flowers; that is ugly.

The original face simply means that you are not being dominated by any kind of morality, religion, society, parents, teachers, priests, not being dominated by anyone. Just living your life according to your own inner sense—you have a sensibility—and you will have the original face.

# THE JOY OF LIVING DANGEROUSLY

*Those who are courageous, they go headlong. They search all opportunities of danger. Their life philosophy is not that of insurance companies. Their life philosophy is that of a mountain climber, a glider, a surfer. And not only in the outside seas they surf; they surf in their innermost seas. And not only on the outside they climb Alps and Himalayas; they seek inner peaks.*

To live dangerously means to live. If you don't live dangerously, you don't live. Living flowers only in danger. Living never flowers in security; it flowers only in insecurity.

If you start getting secure, you become a stagnant pool. Then your energy is no longer moving. Then you are afraid . . . because one never knows how to go into the unknown. And why take the risk? The known is more secure. Then you get obsessed with the familiar. You go on getting fed up with it, you are bored with it, you feel miserable in it, but still it seems familiar and comfortable. At least it is known. The unknown creates a trembling in you. The very idea of the unknown, and you start feeling unsafe.

There are only two types of people in the world. People who want to live comfortably—they are seeking death, they want a comfortable grave. And people who want to live—they choose to live dangerously, because life thrives only when there is risk.

Have you ever gone climbing the mountains? The higher the climb, the fresher you feel, the younger you feel. The greater the danger of falling, the bigger the abyss by the side, the more alive you are . . . between life and death, when you are just hanging between life and death. Then there is no boredom, then there is no dust of the past, no desire for the future. Then the present moment is very sharp, like a flame. It is enough—you live in the here and now.

Or surfing, or skiing, or gliding—wherever there is a risk of losing life, there is tremendous joy because the risk of losing life makes you tremendously alive. Hence people are attracted to dangerous sports.

People go climbing the mountains. . . . Somebody asked Edmund Hillary, "Why did you try to climb Everest? Why?" And Hillary said, "Because it is there—a constant challenge." It was risky, many people had died before. For almost sixty, seventy years, groups had been going—and it was almost a certain death, but still people were going. What was the attraction?

Reaching higher, going farther away from the settled, the routine life, you again become wild, you again become part of the animal world. You again live like a tiger or a lion, or like a river. You again soar like a bird into the skies, farther and farther away. And each moment the security, the bank balance, the wife, the husband, the family, the society, the church, the respectability—all are fading away and away, distant and distant. You become alone.

This is why people are so much interested in sports. But that too is not real danger because you can become very, very skilled. You can learn it, you can be trained for it. It is a very calculated risk—if you allow me the expression, calculated risk. You can train for mountaineering and you can take all the precautions. Or driving at high speeds—you can go a hundred miles per hour and it is dangerous, it is thrilling. But you can become really skillful about it and the danger is only for outsiders; for you it is not. Even if risk is there, it is marginal. And then, these risks are only physical risks, only the body is involved.

When I say to you, live dangerously, I mean not only bodily risk but psychological risk, and finally spiritual risk. Religiousness is spiritual risk. It is going to such heights from where maybe there is no return. That is the meaning of Buddha's term *anagamin*—one who never returns. It is going to such a height, to a point of no return . . . then one is simply lost. One never comes back.

When I say live dangerously, I mean don't live the life of or-dinary respectability—that you are a mayor in a town, or a member of the corporation. This is not life. Or you are a minister, or you have a good profession and are earning well and money goes on accumulating in the bank and everything is going perfectly well. When everything is going perfectly well, simply see it—you are dying and nothing is happening. People may respect you, and when you die a great procession will follow you. Good, that's all, and in the newspapers your pictures will be published and there will be editorials, and then people will forget about you. And you lived your whole life only for these things?

Watch—one can miss one's whole life for ordinary, mundane things. To be spiritual means to understand that these small things should not be given too much importance. I am not saying that they are meaningless. I am saying that they are meaningful but not as meaningful as you think.

Money is needed. It is a need. But money is not the goal and cannot be the goal. A house is needed, certainly. It is a need. I am not an ascetic and I don't want you to destroy your houses and escape to the Himalayas. The house is needed—but the house is needed for you. Don't misunderstand it.

As I see people, the whole thing has gone topsy-turvy. They exist as if they are needed for the house. They go on working for the house. As if they are needed for the bank balance—they simply go on collecting money and then they die. And they had never lived. They had never a single moment of throbbing, streaming life. They were just imprisoned in security, familiarity, respectability.

> I am not an ascetic and I don't want you to destroy your houses and escape to the Himalayas. The house is needed—but the house is needed for you. Don't misunderstand it.

Then if you feel bored, it is natural. People come to me and they say they feel very bored. They feel fed up, stuck, what to do? They think that just by repeating a mantra they will become again alive. It is not so easy. They will have to change their whole life pattern.

Love, but don't think that tomorrow the woman will be available to you. Don't expect. Don't reduce the woman into a wife. Then you are living dangerously. Don't reduce the man into a husband, because a husband is an ugly thing. Let your man be your man and your woman your woman, and don't make your tomorrow predictable. Expect nothing and be ready for everything. That's what I mean when I say live dangerously.

What do we do? We fall in love with a woman and immediately we start going to the court, or to the registry office, or to the church, to get married. I'm not saying don't get married. It is a formality. Good, satisfy the society, but deep in your mind never possess the woman. Never for a single moment say that "you belong to me." Because how can a person belong to you? And when you start possessing the woman, she will start possessing you. Then you both are no longer in love. You are just crushing and killing each other, paralyzing each other.

Love, but don't let your love degrade into marriage. Work—work is needed—but don't let work become your only life. Play should remain your life, your center of life. Work should be just a means toward play.

> Love, but don't think that tomorrow the woman will be available to you. Don't expect. Don't reduce the woman into a wife. Then you are living dangerously.

Work in the office and work in the factory and work in the shop, but just to have time, opportunity, to play. Don't let your life be reduced into just a working routine—because the goal of life is play!

Play means doing something for its own sake. If you enjoy many more things for their own sake, you will be more alive. Of course, your life will always be in risk, in danger. But that's how life has to be. Risk is part of it. In fact the better part of it is risk, the best part of it is risk. The most beautiful part of it is risk. It is every moment a risk. You may not be aware. . . . You breathe in, you breathe out, there is risk. Even breathing out—who knows whether the breath will come back or not? It is not certain, there is no guarantee.

But there are a few people whose whole religion is security. Even if they talk about God, they talk about God as the supreme security. If they think about God, they think only because they are afraid. If they go to pray and meditate, they are going just in order that they remain in the "good books," in God's good books: "If there is a God, he will know that I was a regular churchgoer, a regular worshiper. I can testify to it." Even their prayer is just a means.

To live dangerously means to live life as if each moment is its own end. Each moment has its own intrinsic value, and you are not afraid. You know death is there, and you accept the fact that death is there, and you are not hiding against death. In fact, you go and encounter death. You enjoy those moments of encountering death—physically, psychologically, spiritually.

Enjoying those moments where you come directly in contact with death—where death becomes almost a reality—is what I mean when I say live dangerously.

Those who are courageous, go headlong. They search all opportunities of danger. Their life philosophy is not that of insurance companies. Their life philosophy is that of a mountain climber, a glider, a surfer. And not only in the outside seas they surf; they surf in their innermost seas. And not only on the outside they climb Alps and Himalayas; they seek inner peaks.

But remember one thing: never forget the art of risking—

never, never. Always remain capable of risking. Wherever you can find an opportunity to risk, never miss it, and you will never be a loser. Risk is the only guarantee for being truly alive.

## WHATEVER YOU DO, LIFE IS A MYSTERY

The mind has some difficulty in accepting the idea that there is something that is not explainable. Mind has a very mad urge for everything to be explained . . . if not explained, then at least explained away! Anything that remains a puzzle, a paradox, goes on troubling your mind.

The whole history of philosophy, religion, science, mathematics, has the same root, the same mind—the same itch. You may scratch yourself one way, somebody else may do it differently, but the itch has to be understood. The itch is the belief that existence is not a mystery. Mind can feel at home only if somehow existence is demystified.

Religion has done it by creating God, the Holy Ghost, the Only Begotten Son; different religions have created different things. These are their ways to cover up a hole that is uncoverable; whatever you do the hole is there. In fact the more you cover it, the more emphatically it is there. Your very effort to cover it shows your fear that somebody is going to see the hole.

The whole history of mind, in different branches, has been doing patchwork to conceal this hole—particularly in mathematics, because mathematics is purely a mind game. There are mathematicians who think it is not, just as there are theologians who think God is a reality. God is only an idea. And if horses have ideas, their God will be a horse.

You can be absolutely certain it will not be man, because man has been so cruel to horses that man can be conceived only as a devil, not as God. But then every animal will have its own idea of God, just as every human race has its own idea of God.

Ideas are substitutes for where life is mysterious and you find gaps that cannot be filled by reality. You fill those gaps with ideas; and at least you start feeling satisfied that life is understood.

Have you ever thought about this word *understand*? It means standing under you. It is strange that this word has by and by taken a meaning that is far from the original idea: anything that you can make stand under you, that is under your thumb, under your power, under your shoe, you are the master of.

People have been trying to understand life in that same way, so that they could put life also underneath their feet and declare, "We are the masters. Now there is nothing which is not understood by us."

> Ideas are substitutes for where life is mysterious and you find gaps that cannot be filled by reality. You fill those gaps with ideas, and at least you start feeling satisfied that life is understood.

But it is not possible. Whatever you do, life is a mystery and is going to remain a mystery.

THERE IS A BEYOND EVERYWHERE. We are surrounded by the beyond. That beyond is what God is; that beyond has to be penetrated. It is within, it is without; it is always there. And if you forget about it . . . as we do ordinarily, because it is very uncomfortable, inconvenient, to look into the beyond. It is as if one looks into an abyss, and one starts trembling, one starts feeling sick. The very awareness of the abyss and you start trembling. Nobody looks at the abyss; we go on looking in other directions, we go on avoiding the real. The real *is* like an abyss, because the real is a great emptiness. It is vast sky with no boundaries. Buddha says: *Durangama*—be available to the beyond. Never remain confined to the boundaries, always trespass boundaries. Make the boundaries if you need them, but always remember you have to step out. Never make imprisonments.

We make many sorts of imprisonments: relationship, belief, religion—they are all imprisonments. One feels cozy because there are no wild winds blowing. One feels protected—although the protection is false, because death will come and will drag you into the beyond. Before death comes and drags you into the beyond, go on your own.

A story:

A Zen monk was going to die. He was very old, ninety years old. Suddenly he opened his eyes and he said, "Where are my shoes?"

And the disciple said, "Where are you going? Have you gone crazy? You are dying, and the physician has said that there is no more possibility; a few minutes more."

He said, "That's why I'm asking for my shoes: I would like to go to the cemetery, because I don't want to be dragged. I will walk on my own and I will meet death there. I don't want to be dragged. And you know me—I have never leaned on anybody else. This will be very ugly, that four persons will be carrying me. No."

He walked to the cemetery. Not only that, he dug his own grave, lay down in it, and died. Such courage to accept the unknown, such courage to go on your own and welcome the beyond! Then death is transformed, then death is no longer death.

Such a courageous man never dies; death is defeated. Such a courageous man goes beyond death. For one who goes on his own to the beyond, the beyond is never like death. Then the beyond becomes a welcome. If you welcome the beyond, the beyond welcomes you; the beyond always goes on echoing you.

## LIFE IS ALWAYS IN THE WILD

Ego surrounds you like a wall. It persuades you that by surrounding you in this way it will protect you. That's the seduction of the ego. It goes on telling you again and again, "If I am not there you will be unprotected, you will become too vulnerable, and there will be too much risk. So let me guard you, let me surround you."

Yes, there is a certain protection in the ego, but the wall becomes your imprisonment also. There is a certain protection, otherwise nobody would suffer the miseries that ego brings. There is a certain protection, it protects you against the enemy—but then it protects you against the friends also.

It is just like when you close your door and hide behind it because you are afraid of the enemy. Then a friend comes but the door is closed, he cannot enter. If you are too afraid of the enemy then the friend also cannot enter into you. And if you open the door for the friend, there is every risk that the enemy may also enter.

One has to think about it deeply; it is one of the greatest problems in life. And only a very few courageous people tackle it rightly; others become cowards and hide and then their whole life is lost.

Life is risky, death has no risk. Die, and then there is no problem for you and nobody is going to kill you because how can anybody kill you when you are already dead? Enter a grave and be finished! Then there is no illness, then there is no anxiety, then there is no problem—you are out of all problems.

But if you are alive, then there are millions of problems. The more alive the person, the more problems there are. But there is nothing wrong in it because struggling with problems, fighting with the challenge, is how you grow.

The ego is a subtle wall around you. It does not allow anybody to enter into you. You feel protected, secure, but this security is deathlike. It is the security of the plant inside the seed. The plant is afraid to sprout because who knows?—the world is so hazardous and the plant will be so soft, so fragile. Behind the wall of the seed, hiding inside the cell, everything is protected.

Or think of a small child in the mother's womb. Everything is there, whatsoever the need of the child it is fulfilled immediately. There is no anxiety, no fight, no future. The child simply lives blissfully. Every need is fulfilled by the mother.

> The more alive the person, the more problems there are. But there is nothing wrong in it because struggling with problems, fighting with the challenge, is how you grow.

But would you like to remain always in your mother's womb? It is very protective. If it was given to you to choose, would you choose always to be in the mother's womb? It is very comfortable, what more comfort is possible? Scientists say that we have not yet been able to make a situation more comfortable than the womb. The womb seems to be the last, the ultimate in comfort. So comfortable—no anxiety, no problem, no need to work. Sheer existence. And everything is supplied automatically—the need arises and immediately it is supplied. There is not even the trouble of breathing—the mother breathes for the child. There is no bother about food—the mother eats for the child.

But would you like to remain in the mother's womb? It is comfortable but it is not life. Life is always in the wild. Life is there outside.

The English word *ecstasy* is very, very significant. It means to stand out. Ecstasy means to get out—out of all shells and all protections and all egos and all comforts, all deathlike walls. To be ecstatic means to get out, to be free, to be moving, to be a process, to be vulnerable so that winds can come and pass through you.

We have an expression, sometimes we say, "That experience was outstanding." That exactly is the meaning of ecstasy: outstanding.

When a seed breaks and the light hidden within starts manifesting, when a child is born and leaves the womb behind, all the comforts and all the conveniences behind, moves into the unknown world—it is ecstasy. When a bird breaks the egg and flies into the sky, it is ecstasy.

The ego is the egg, and you will have to come out of it. Be ecstatic! Get out of all protections and shells and securities. Then you will attain to the wider world, the vast, the infinite. Only then you live, and you live abundantly.

But fear cripples you. The child, before he gets out of the womb, must also be hesitating about whether to get out or not. To be or not to be? It must take one step forward and another step back. Maybe that's why the mother goes through so much pain. The child is hesitating, the child is not yet totally ready to be ecstatic. The past pulls it back, the future calls it forth, and the child is divided.

This is the wall of indecision, of clinging with the past, of clinging with the ego. And you carry it everywhere. Sometimes, in rare moments, when you are very alive and alert, you will be able to see it. Otherwise, although it is a very transparent wall, you will not be able to see it. One can live his whole life—and not one life, many—without becoming aware that one is living inside a cell, closed from everywhere, windowless, what Leibnitz used to call "monad." No doors, no windows, just closed inside—but it is transparent, a glass wall.

This ego has to be dropped. One has to gather courage and shatter it on the floor. People go on feeding it in millions of ways, not knowing that they feed their own hell.


Mrs. Cochrane was standing beside the coffin of her dead husband. Their son stood at her elbow. The mourners, one by one, passed in review.

"He's feeling no pain now," said Mrs. Croy. "What did he die of?"

"Poor fella," said Mrs. Cochrane. "He died of gonorrhea!"

Another woman gazed at the corpse. "He's well out of it now," she said. "He's got a smile of serenity on his face. What did he die from?"

"He died of gonorrhea!" said the widow.

Suddenly, the son pulled the mother aside. "Mom," he said, "that's a terrible thing to say about Pop. He didn't die of gonorrhea. He died of diarrhea!"

"I know that!" said Mrs. Cochrane. "But I'd rather have them thinkin' he died like a sport, instead of the shit he was!"

To the very end they go on playing games.

The ego does not allow you to be true, it goes on forcing you to be false. The ego is the lie, but that one has to decide. It needs great courage because with it will shatter all that you have been nursing up to now. It will shatter your whole past. With it *you* will shatter completely. Somebody will be there but you will not be that person. A discontinuous entity will arise within you—fresh, uncorrupted by the past. Then there will be no wall; then wherever you will be, you will see the infinite without any boundaries.

The old man, entering his favorite bar, found that the usual barmaid had been replaced by a stranger. He was nonplussed at first but gallantly told her that she was "the best-looking girl I've seen in a long time."

The new barmaid, a haughty type, tossed her head and replied acidly, "I'm sorry I can't return the compliment."

"Oh, well, my dear," the old man answered placidly, "couldn't you have done as I did? Couldn't you have told a lie?"

All our formalities are nothing but helping each other's ego. They *are* lies. You say something to somebody and he returns the compliment. Neither you nor he is true. We go on playing the game: etiquette, formalities, the civilized faces and masks.

Then you will have to face the wall. And by and by, the wall will become so thick that you will not be able to see anything. The wall goes on getting more and more thick every day—so don't wait. If you have come to feel that you are carrying a wall around you, drop it! Jump out of it! It takes only a decision to jump out of it, nothing else. Then from tomorrow don't feed it. Then whenever you see that you are again nursing it, stop. Within a few days you will see it has died, because it needs your constant support, it needs breastfeeding.

> This ego has to be dropped. One has to gather courage and shatter it on the floor. People go on feeding it in millions of ways, not knowing that they feed their own hell.

# THE ULTIMATE COURAGE: NO BEGINNING, NO END

There are many fears, but fundamentally they are only offshoots of one fear, branches of one tree. The name of the tree is death. You may not be aware that this fear is concerned with death, but every fear is concerned with death.

Fear is only a shadow. It may not be apparent if you are afraid of going bankrupt, but you are really afraid of being without money and becoming more vulnerable to death. People go on holding money as a protection, although they know perfectly well that there is no way to protect yourself against death. But still, something has to be done. At least it keeps you busy, and keeping yourself busy is a kind of unconsciousness, is a kind of drug.

Hence, just as there are alcoholics, there are workaholics. They keep themselves continuously involved in some work; they cannot leave working. Holidays are fearful; they cannot sit silently. They may start reading the same newspapers they have read three times already that morning. They want to remain engaged, because it keeps a curtain between themselves and death. But reduced to its essentials, the only fear is of death.

It is significant to realize that all other fears are only offshoots, because then something can be done if you know the very roots. If death is the basic and the fundamental fear, then only one thing can make you fearless, and that is an experience within you of a deathless consciousness. Nothing else—no money, no power, no prestige—nothing can be an insurance against death except a deep meditation . . . which reveals to you that your body will die, your mind will die, but you are beyond the body-mind structure. Your essential core, your essential life source has been here before you and will remain after you. It has changed through many forms; it has evolved through many forms. But it has never disappeared, from the very beginning—if there has been any beginning. And it will never disappear to the very end, if there is any end . . . because I don't believe in any beginning and in any end.

Existence is beginningless and endless. It has always been here and you have always been here. Forms may have been different; forms have been different even in this life.

The first day you got into your mother's womb, you were not bigger than the dot on your question mark. If a photograph is shown to you, you will not recognize that this is you. And in fact, even before that . . .

Two persons were arguing about how far back they could go, how far back they could remember. One could remember his childhood nearabout three years of age. The other said, "That's nothing. I remember the day my mother and father went to a picnic. When we went to the picnic, I was in the father. When we came back from the picnic I was in my mother!"

Will you recognize yourself as you were when you were in your father? A picture can be shown to you; it can be enlarged so that you can see it with your bare eyes, but you will not recognize it. But it is the same life-form, the same life source that is throbbing in you right now.

You are changing every day. When you were just born, just one day old, that also you will not be able to recognize. You will say, "My god, this is me?" Everything will change; you will become old, youth will be gone. Childhood has been lost long before, and death will come. But it will come only to the form, not to the essence. And what has been changing all along your life was only the form.

Your form is changing every moment. And death is nothing but a change, a vital change, a little bigger change, a quicker change. From childhood to youth . . . you don't recognize when childhood left you and you became young. From youth to old age . . . things go so gradually that you never recognize at what date, on what day, in what year, youth left you. The change is very gradual and slow.

Death is a quantum jump from one body, from one form into another form. But it is not an end to you.

You were never born and you never die.

You are always here. Forms come and go and the river of life continues. Unless you experience this, the fear of death will not leave you. Only meditation . . . only meditation can help.

I can say it; all the scriptures can say it, but that will not help; still a doubt may remain. Who knows, these people may have been lying, or these people may have been deceived themselves. Or these people may have been deceived by other literature, by other teachers. And if a doubt remains, the fear will be there.

Meditation brings you face to face with the reality.

Once you know on your own what life is, you never bother about death.

You can go beyond. . . . It is within your power and it is your right. But you will have to make the small effort of moving from mind to no-mind.

THE MOMENT THE CHILD IS BORN, YOU THINK, IS THE BE-
GINNING OF ITS LIFE. That is not true. The moment an old man
dies, you think, is the end of his life. It is not. Life is far bigger than
birth and death. Birth and death are not two ends of life; many
births and many deaths happen within life. Life itself has no beginning, no end; life and eternity are equivalent. But you cannot understand very easily how life can turn
into death; even to concede that is
impossible.

There are a few inconceivables
in the world, and one of them is you
cannot conceive of life turning into
death. At what point is it no longer
life and it becomes death? Where will
you mark the line? Neither can you
mark the line for birth, when life begins: is it when the child is born or
when the child is conceived? But
even before conception the mother's
egg was alive, the father's sperm was
alive—they were not dead, because
the meeting of two dead things cannot create life. At what point is
the child born? Science has not been able to decide. There is no
way to decide, because the eggs that the mother is carrying she has
been carrying from her birth. . . .

> Death is a quantum
> jump from one body,
> from one form into
> another form.
> But it is not an end
> to you.
> You were never born
> and you never die.
> You are always here.

One thing has to be accepted, that half of your being is alive
in your mother, even before you are conceived. And half of you is
to be contributed by your father—that too has to be contributed

alive. When the sperms leave your father's body they are alive—but they don't have a long life, they have only two hours' life. Within two hours they have to meet the mother's egg. If within two hours they don't meet, if they start bumming around here and there. . . .

It is absolutely certain that each sperm must have its own characteristic personality. A few are lazy fellows; when others are running toward the egg, they are just taking a morning walk. This way they are never going to reach, but what can they do? These characteristics are present from their birth: they cannot run, they would prefer to die; and they are not even aware what is going to happen.

But a few guys are just Olympic racers, they immediately start running fast. And there is great competition because it is not a question of a few hundred cells running toward the mother's single egg. . . . The mother has a reservoir of eggs, which is limited and which releases only one egg every month. That's why she has the monthly period; every month one egg is released. So only one fellow out of this whole mob, which consists of millions of living cells . . . it is really a great philosophical problem!

It is nothing, just biology, because the problem is that out of so many millions of people, only one person can be born. And who were those other millions that could not get into the mother's egg? This has been used as one of the arguments in India by Hindu scholars, pundits, *shankaracharyas*, against birth control.

India is clever about argumentation. The pope goes on talking against birth control but has not produced a single argument. At least the Indian counterpart has produced a few very valid-looking arguments. One of their arguments is: At what point to stop producing children?—two children, three children? They say that Rabindranath

Tagore was the thirteenth child of his parents; if birth control had been practiced there would have been no Rabindranath.

The argument seems to be valid because birth control means stopping at two children, at the most three: don't take any chance, one may die or something may happen. You can reproduce two children to replace you and your wife, so no population increase happens; but Rabindranath was the thirteenth child of his parents. If they had stopped even at one dozen then too Rabindranath would have missed the train. Now how many Rabindranaths are missing trains?

I was talking to one of the *shankaracharyas*. I said, "Perfectly right; for argument's sake I accept that this is true: we would have missed one Rabindranath Tagore. But I am willing to miss him. If the whole country can live peacefully, can have enough food, can have enough clothes, can have all basic needs fulfilled, I think it is worth it. I am ready to lose one Rabindranath Tagore, it is nothing much. You have to see the balance: millions of people dying and starving just to produce one Rabindranath Tagore? So you mean every parent has to go up to thirteen? But what about the fourteenth? What about the fifteenth?"

And forget about these small numbers; in each lovemaking a man releases millions of sperms—and every time a man makes love a child is not conceived. Millions of people in each lovemaking simply disappear. We will never know how many Nobel prize winners were there, how many presidents, prime ministers . . . all kinds of people must have been there.

So this is my calculation: from the fourteenth year to the age of forty-two, if a man goes absolutely normally about his lovemaking, he will release almost the equal amount of sperms as is the whole population of the earth. A single man can populate the whole earth—overpopulate it!—it is already overpopulated. And all these people will be unique individuals, not having anything in common except their humanness.

No, life does not start there either; life starts farther back. But to you that is only a hypothesis—to me it is an experience. Life begins at the point of your past life's death. When you die, on the one side one chapter of life—which people think was your whole life—is closed. It was only a chapter in a book that has infinite chapters. One chapter closes, but the book is not closed. Just turn the page and another chapter begins.

The person dying starts visualizing his next life. This is a known fact, because it happens before the chapter closes. Once in a while a person comes back from the very last point. For example he is drowning, and he is somehow saved. He is almost in a coma; the water has to be taken out, artificial breathing has to be given, and somehow he is saved. He was just on the verge of closing the chapter. These people have reported interesting facts.

One is that at the last moment when they felt that they were dying, that it was finished, their whole past life went fast before them, in a flash—from birth to that moment. Within a split second they saw everything that had happened to them, that they had remembered, and also that which they had never remembered; many things that they had not even taken note of and that they were not aware were part of their memory. The whole film of memory goes so quickly, in a flash—and it has to be in a split second because the man is dying, there is no time, like three hours to see the whole movie.

And even if you see the whole movie you cannot relate the whole story of a man's life with small, insignificant details. But everything passes before him—that is a certain, very significant phenomenon. Before ending the chapter he recollects all his experiences, unfulfilled desires, expectations, disappointments, frustrations, sufferings, joys—everything.

Buddha has a word for it, he calls it *tanha*. Literally it means desire, but metaphorically it means the whole life of desire. All these things happened—frustrations, fulfillments, disappointments, successes, failures—but all this happened within a certain arena you can call desire.

The dying man has to see the whole of it before he moves on farther, just to recollect it, because the body is going: this mind is not going to be with him, this brain is not going to be with him. But the desire released from this mind will cling to his soul, and this desire will decide his future life. Whatever has remained unfulfilled, he will move toward that target.

Your life begins far back before your birth, before your mother's impregnation, farther back, in your past life's end. That end is the beginning of this life. One chapter closes, another chapter opens. Now, how this new life will be is ninety-nine percent determined by the last moment of your death. What you collected, what you have brought with you like a seed—that seed will become a tree, bring fruits, bring flowers, or whatever happens to it. You cannot read it in the seed, but the seed has the whole blueprint.

There is a possibility that one day science may be able to read the whole program in the seed—what kind of branches this tree is going to have, how long this tree is going to live, what is going to happen to this tree. Because the blueprint is there, we just don't know the language. Everything that is going to happen is already potentially present.

So what you do at the moment of your death determines how your birth is going to be. Most people die clinging. They don't want to die, and one can understand why they don't want to die. Only at the moment of death do they recognize the fact that they have not lived. Life has simply passed as if a dream, and death has come. Now there is no more time to live—death is knocking on the door. And when there was time to live, you were doing a thousand and one foolish things, wasting your time rather than living it.

> ❧
>
> Most people die clinging. They don't want to die, and one can understand why they don't want to die. Only at the moment of death do they recognize the fact that they have not lived.

I have asked people playing cards, playing chess, "What are you doing?"

They say, "Killing time."

From my very childhood I have been against this expression, "killing time." My grandfather was a great chess player, and I would ask him, "You are getting old and you are still killing time. Can't you see that really time is killing you? And you go on saying that you are killing time. You don't know even what time is, you don't know where it is. Just catch hold of it and show me."

All these expressions that time is fleeting, and passing, and going, are just a kind of consolation. It is really you who are passing—going down the drain every moment. And you go on thinking it is time that is passing, as if you are going to stay and time is going to pass! Time is where it is; it is not passing. Watches and clocks are man's creation to measure the passing time, which is not passing at all.

In India, in Punjab, if you are traveling in Punjab never ask anybody, "What is the time?" because if it happens to be twelve you will be beaten and if you can escape alive it will be just a miracle. It is just for a very philosophical reason—but when philosophy comes into the hands of fools, this is what happens.

Nanak, the founder of Sikhism, has said that the moment of samadhi, enlightenment, is just like two hands of the clock meeting on twelve, where they are no longer two. He was just taking an example—that in the moment of samadhi the twoness of your being dissolves and you arrive at oneness. The same happens in death too. He explained later on that the same happens in death: again the two hands that have been separately moving come together and stop, become one: you become one with existence.

So in Punjab, twelve o'clock has become the symbol of death. So if you ask any sardarji, "What is the time?" if it happens to be twelve, he will simply start beating you, because that means you are teasing him, and you are cursing him with death. About somebody with a long face, miserable, in anguish, in Punjab they will say, "On his face it is twelve o'clock." I have seen sardars changing their watch quickly: when it comes to twelve they will move it five minutes ahead quickly. They won't keep it on twelve; it hurts that their own watch is playing tricks on them. Twelve reminds them only of misery, sadness, death; they have completely forgotten about samadhi, which Nanak was really trying to explain to them.

When a person dies—when it is twelve o'clock for him—he clings to life. His whole life he has been thinking time is passing;

now he feels he is going, he has passed. No clinging can help. He becomes so miserable, and the misery becomes so unbearable that most people fall into a kind of unconscious state, a coma, before they die. So they miss recollecting their whole life.

If death is without any clinging, if there is no desire to remain alive even for a single moment more, you will die consciously because there is no need for nature to make you unconscious or force you into a coma. You will die alert, and you will recollect the whole past. You will be able to see that whatever you have been doing was simply stupid.

> ☞
>
> If death is without any clinging, if there is no desire to remain alive even for a single moment more, you will die consciously because there is no need for nature to make you unconscious or force you into a coma.

Desires have been fulfilled— what have you gained? Desires have remained unfulfilled and you have suffered, but what have you gained when they are fulfilled? It is a strange game in which you are always losing, whether you win or lose makes no difference.

Your pleasures were nothing, just signatures made on water, and your pain was engraved on granite. And you suffered all that pain for these signatures on water. You suffered your whole life for small joys that don't appear to be more than toys at this stage, from this height, from this point where you can see the whole valley of your life. Successes were also failures.

Failures of course were failures, and pleasures were nothing but incentives to suffer pain.

All your euphoria was just the function of your dream faculty. You are going with empty hands. This whole life has been just a vicious circle: you went on moving in the same circle, around and around and around. And you have not arrived anywhere because by moving in a circle, how you can arrive anywhere? The center always remained at the same distance, wherever you were on the circle.

Success came, failure came; pleasure came, pain came; there was misery and there was joy. Everything went on happening on the circle, but the center of your being always remained equidistant from every place. It was difficult to see while you were in the circle—you were too much involved in it, too much part of it. But now, suddenly all has dropped out of your hands—you are standing empty.

Kahlil Gibran, in his masterpiece, *The Prophet*, has one sentence. . . . Al-Mustafa, the prophet, comes running to the people who are working in the farms and says to them, "My ship has arrived, my time has come to go. I have come here just to glance back on all that has happened and on all that has not happened. Before I go aboard the ship I have a great longing just to see what my life here was."

The sentence that I was going to remind you of is . . . he says, "I am just like a river which is going to fall into the ocean. She waits for a moment to look back at the whole terrain that she has passed—the jungles, the mountains, the people. It has been a rich life of thousands of miles, and now, in a single moment, all is going to dissolve. So just like a river on the brink of falling into the ocean looks back, I want to look back."

But this looking back is possible only if you are not clinging to the past; otherwise you are so afraid to lose it that you don't have time to observe, to see. And time is just a split second. If a man dies fully alert, seeing the whole terrain that he has passed and seeing the whole stupidity of it, he is born with a sharpness, with an intelligence, with courage—automatically. It is not something he does.

People ask me, "You were sharp, courageous, intelligent, even as an infant; I am not that courageous even now. . . ." The reason is that I died in my past life in a different way than you died. That makes the great difference, because the way you die, in the same way you are born. Your death is one side of the coin, your birth is another side of the same coin.

If on the other side there was confusion, misery, anguish, clinging, desire, then on this side of the coin you can't expect sharpness, intelligence, courage, clarity, awareness. That will be absolutely unwarranted; you cannot expect that.

That's why it is very simple but difficult to explain to you, because I have not done anything in this life to be courageous or to be sharp and intelligent from the very beginning. And I have never thought about it as courage or sharpness or intelligence.

It was only later on that slowly I became aware of how stupid people are. It was only a later reflection; earlier I was not aware that I was courageous. I was thinking everybody must be the same. Only later on it became clear to me that everybody is not the same.

As I started growing up I started becoming aware of my past life, and death, and I remembered how easily I had died—not only easily but enthusiastically. My interest was more in knowing the unknown that was ahead than in the known that I had seen. I have never looked back. And this has been my whole life's way—not to look back. There is no point. You can't go back, so why waste time? I am always looking ahead. Even at the point of death I was looking ahead—and that's what made me clear why I was missing the brakes that prevent other people from doing things.

Those brakes are provided by your fear of the unknown. You are clinging to the past and you are afraid to move into the unknown. You are clinging to the known, the acquainted. It may be painful, it may be ugly, but at least you know it. You have grown a certain kind of friendship with it.

You will be surprised, but this is my experience of thousands of people: they cling to their misery for the simple reason that they have grown a certain kind of friendship with misery. They have lived with it so long that now to leave it will be almost like a divorce.

The same is the situation with marriage and divorce. The man thinks at least twelve times in a day about divorce; the woman thinks also—but somehow both go on managing, living together for the simple reason that both are afraid of the unknown. This man is bad, okay, but who knows about the other man?—he may prove worse. And at least you have become accustomed to this man's

> This is my experience of thousands of people: they cling to their misery for the simple reason that they have grown a certain kind of friendship with misery. They have lived with it so long that now to leave it will be almost like a divorce.

badness, unlovingness, and you can tolerate it. You have tolerated it, you have also become thick-skinned. With the new man, you never know; you will have to start from the very scratch again. So people go on clinging to the known.

Just watch people at the moment of death. Their suffering is not death. Death has no pain in it, it is absolutely painless. It is really pleasant; it is just like a deep sleep. Do you think deep sleep is something painful? But they are not concerned about death, and deep sleep, and pleasure; they are worried about the known that is slipping out of their hands. Fear means only one thing: losing the known and entering into the unknown.

Courage is just the opposite of fear.

Always be ready to drop the known—more than willing to drop it—not even waiting for it to be ripe. Just jump on something that is new . . . its very newness, its very freshness, is so alluring. Then there is courage.

The fear of death is certainly the greatest fear and the most destructive of your courage.

So I can suggest only one thing. Now you cannot go back to your past death, but you can start doing one thing: Always be ready to move from the known to the unknown, in anything, any experience.

It is better, even if the unknown proves worse than the known—that is not the point. Just your change from the known to the unknown, your readiness to move from the known to the unknown, is what matters. It is immensely valuable. And in all kinds of experiences, go on doing that. That will prepare you for death, because when death comes you cannot suddenly decide, "I choose death and leave life." These decisions are not made suddenly.

You have to go inch by inch, preparing, living moment to moment. And as you grow more familiar with the beauty of the unknown, you start creating a new quality in you. It is there, it has just never been used. Before death comes, go on moving from the known to the unknown. Always remember that the new is better than the old.

They say all that is old is not gold. I say, even if all that is old is gold, forget about it. Choose the new—gold or no gold, it doesn't matter. What matters is your choice: your choice to learn, your choice to experience, your choice to go into the dark. Slowly slowly your courage will start functioning. And sharpness of intelligence is not something separate from courage, it is almost one organic whole.

> Even if all that is old is gold, forget about it.
> Choose the new—gold or no gold, it doesn't matter.

With fear there is cowardliness and there is bound to be retardedness of the mind, mediocrity. They are all together, they support each other. With courage comes sharpness, intelligence, openness, an unprejudiced mind, the capacity to learn—they all come together.

Start with a simple exercise: always remember, whenever there is a choice, choose the unknown, the risky, the dangerous, the insecure, and you will not be at a loss.

And only then . . . this time death can become a tremendously revealing experience and can give you the insight into your new birth—not only insight but even a certain choice. With awareness you can choose a certain mother, a certain father. Ordinarily it is all unconscious, just accidental, but a man dying with awareness is born with awareness.

You can ask my mother something—because she happens to be here. . . . After my birth, for three days I didn't take any milk, and they were all worried, concerned. The doctors were concerned, because how was this child going to survive if he simply refused to take milk? But they had no idea of my difficulty, of what difficulty they were creating for me. They were trying to force me in every possible way. And there was no way I could explain to them, or that they could find out by themselves.

> Always remember, whenever there is a choice, choose the unknown, the risky, the dangerous, the insecure, and you will not be at a loss.

In my past life, before I died, I was on a fast. I wanted to complete a twenty-one day fast, but I was murdered before my fast was complete, three days before. Those three days remained in my awareness even in this birth; I had to complete my fast. I am really stubborn! Otherwise, people don't carry things from one life to another life; once a chapter is closed, it is closed.

But for three days they could not manage to put anything in my mouth; I simply rejected it. But after three days I was perfectly okay and they were all surprised: "Why was he refusing for three days? There was no sickness, no problem—and after three days he is perfectly normal." It remained a mystery to them. But these things I don't want to talk about because to you they will all be hypo-thetical, and there is no way for me to prove them scientifically.

And I don't want to give you any belief, so go on cutting all that may create any belief system in your mind.

You love me, you trust me, so whatever I say you may trust it. But I insist, again and again, that anything that is not based on your experience, accept it only hypothetically. Don't make it your belief. If sometimes I give an example, that is sheer necessity— because the people have asked, "How did you manage to be so courageous and sharp in your childhood?"

I have not done anything, I have simply continued what I was doing in my past life.

Courage will come to you.

Just start with a simple formula: *Never miss the unknown*.

Always choose the unknown and go headlong. Even if you suffer, it is worth it—it always pays. You always come out of it more grown up, more mature, more intelligent.

# IN SEARCH OF
# FEARLESSNESS

## Meditation Techniques and Responses to Questions

*Everybody is afraid—has to be. Life is such that one has to be.*
*And people who become fearless, become fearless not by becoming*
*brave—because a brave man has only repressed his fear; he's not*
*really fearless. A man becomes fearless by accepting his fears. It is*
*not a question of bravery. It is simply seeing into the facts of life*
*and realizing that these fears are natural. One accepts them!*

### Are fear and guilt the same thing?

Fear and guilt are not the same thing. Fear accepted becomes
freedom; fear denied, rejected, condemned, becomes guilt. If
you accept fear as part of the situation. . . .

It is part of the situation. Man is a part, a very small, tiny part,
and the whole is vast: a drop, a very small drop, and the whole is
the whole ocean. A trembling arises: "I may be lost in the whole;
my identity may be lost." That is the fear of death. All fear is the
fear of death. And the fear of death is the fear of annihilation.

It is natural that man is afraid, trembling. If you accept it, if you say that this is how life is, if you accept it totally, trembling stops immediately, and fear—the same energy that was becoming fear—uncoils and becomes freedom. Then you know that even if the drop disappears in the ocean, it will be there. In fact, it will become the whole ocean. Then death becomes nirvana, then you are not afraid to lose yourself. Then you understand the saying of Jesus: "If you save your life you will lose it, and if you lose it you will save it."

The only way to go beyond death is to accept death. Then it disappears. The only way to be fearless is to accept fear. Then the energy is released and becomes freedom. But if you condemn it, if you suppress it, if you hide the fact that you are afraid—if you armor yourself and protect yourself and are defensive—then guilt arises.

Anything repressed creates guilt; anything not allowed creates guilt; anything against nature creates guilt. Then you feel guilty that you have been lying to others and lying to yourself. That inauthenticity is guilt.

You ask: "Are fear and guilt the same thing?" No. Fear can be guilt, but it may not be. It depends what you do with fear. If you do something wrong with it, it becomes guilt. If you simply accept it and don't do anything about it—there is nothing to do!—then it becomes freedom, it becomes fearlessness.

Don't say to yourself that you are ugly, wrong, a sinner. Don't condemn. Whatsoever you are, you are. Don't be guilty, don't feel guilty. Even if there is something wrong, *you* are not wrong. Maybe you have acted wrongly, but your being is not wrong because of that. Some action may be wrong, but the being is always right.

*I've noticed about myself that I am always trying to convince others that I'm important and powerful. I meditated on the reasons for this, and I think it's fear.*

The ego is always coming out of fear. A really fearless person has no ego. The ego is a protection, an armor. Because you are afraid, you create an impression around you that you are so-and-so and this and that, mm? So nobody dares to harm you; otherwise it is basically fear. Good! You looked into it deeply and rightly. And once you see the basic cause, things become very simple. Otherwise people go on fighting with the ego—and the ego is not a real problem. So you are fighting with a symptom, not with the real disease. The real disease is fear. You can go on fighting with the ego and you will go on missing the target because the ego is not the real enemy, it is bogus. Even if you win, you will not win anything. And you cannot win—only a real enemy can be defeated, not a false enemy that does not exist at all. It is a facade. It is as if you have a wound and it looks ugly and you put some ornament on it.

> ⤝
>
> The only way to go beyond death is to accept death.
> Then it disappears.
> The only way to be fearless is to accept fear.
> Then the energy is released and becomes freedom.

Once it happened that I was staying at a film star's house and he had asked many people to come and see me. A film actress was also there and she had a really beautiful watch with a beautiful and very big band. Somebody who was sitting by her side started asking about the watch and she became a little worried. I was simply watching. He wanted to see the watch—and she was not willing to take it off. But the man insisted and she had to take it off. Then I could see what was the problem. She had a big white spot, a leprosy spot. She was hiding that leprosy spot under the band of that beautiful watch. Now she was exposed—and she started perspiring and became so nervous. . . .

The ego is just like that. There is fear but nobody wants to show his fear, because if you show that you are afraid many people will be there who will make you more afraid. Once they come to know that you are in deep fear, then everybody will hit you hard. They will enjoy humiliating you, finding that someone is weaker. People enjoy exploiting, kicking that person. . . .

So every person who is afraid, deep down creates a big ego around the fear and goes on pumping more air in that balloon of the ego and becomes too big. Adolf Hitler, Idi Amin of Uganda— that type of person becomes very puffed up. Then he starts making others afraid. Anybody who tries to make anybody afraid, know well that he must himself be deep down afraid, otherwise why? What is the point? Who bothers to make you afraid if he is not afraid?

People full of fear make others afraid so they can rest at ease. They know well that now you will not touch them, you will not trespass their boundaries.

You looked well—that is exactly the case. So don't fight with the ego. Rather, watch fear and try to accept it. It is natural, it is part of life. There is no need to hide it; there is no need to pretend otherwise. It is there—all human beings are full of fear. It is part of humanity. Accept it, and the moment you accept it the ego will disappear, because then there is no point for the ego to be there. Fighting with the ego will not help; accepting the fear will immediately help. Then you know that yes, we are so tiny in such a vast universe—how is it possible not to be afraid? And life is surrounded by death—how is it possible not to be afraid? Any moment we can disappear—a small thing goes wrong and we disappear—so how is it possible not to be afraid? When you accept, by and by fear disappears because now there is no point. You accept it, you have taken it for granted—it is so!

> ≈
>
> People full of fear make others afraid so they can rest at ease. They know well that now you will not touch them, you will not trespass their boundaries.

So don't create something against it to hide it. And when you don't create anything against it, it simply subsides. I'm not saying you will not have any fear, I am saying that you will not be afraid. Fear will be there, but you will not be afraid. You follow me? To be afraid means that you are against fear—you don't want it to be there, and it is there.

When you accept it. . . . Just as trees are green, humanity is full of fear. Then what to do? Trees are not hiding. Everybody is prone to die. Fear is the shadow of death. Accept it!

*When I am by myself I feel I can let go in some ways and love people, but as soon as I come into their presence, the shutters go up.*

It is difficult to love real people because a real person is not going to fulfill your expectations. He is not meant to. He is not here to fulfill anybody else's expectations; he has to live his own life. And whenever he moves somewhere that goes against you or is not in tune with your feelings, emotions, your being, it becomes difficult.

It is very easy to think about love. It is very difficult to love. It is very easy to love the whole world. The real difficulty is to love a single human being. It is very easy to love God or humanity. The real problem arises when you come across a real person and you encounter him. To encounter him is to go through a great change and a great challenge.

> It is very easy to think about love. It is very difficult to love. It is very easy to love the whole world. The real difficulty is to love a single human being.

He is not going to be your slave and neither are you going to be a slave to him. That's where the real problem arises. If you are going to be a slave or if he is going to be a slave, then there is no problem. The problem arises because nobody is here to play a slave—and nobody can be a slave. Everybody is a free agent . . . the whole being consists of freedom. Man is freedom.

So remember, the problem is real, it has nothing to do with you personally. The problem has to do with the whole phenomenon of love. Don't make it a personal problem, otherwise you will be in difficulty. Everybody has to face the same problem, more or less. I have never come across a person who has no difficulty in love. It has something to do with love, the very world of love.

The very relationship brings you to such situations where problems arise, and it is good to pass through them. In the East people have escaped, just seeing the difficulty in it. They started denying their love, rejecting their love. They became loveless and they called it nonattachment. By and by they became deadened. Love almost disappeared from the East and only meditation remained.

Meditation means that you are feeling good in your loneliness. Meditation means that you are related only to yourself. Your circle is complete with yourself; you don't go out of it. Of course ninety-nine percent of your problems are solved—but at a very great cost. You will be less troubled now. The eastern man is less anxious, less tense, almost lives in his own inner cave, protected, with eyes closed. He does not allow his energy to move. He makes a short circuit, a small energy movement inside his being, and he is happy. But his happiness is a little dead. His happiness is not a jubilation, it is not a joy.

At the most you can say that it is not unhappiness. At the most you can say something of the negative about it, as if you say that you are healthy because you don't have any illness. But that is not much of a health. Health should have something positive, a glow of its own—not just absence of disease. In that way even a dead body is healthy because it has no illnesses.

So in the East we have tried to live without love, to renounce the world—that means to renounce love—to renounce the woman, the man, and all possibilities where love can flower. Jain monks, Hindu monks, Buddhist monks, are not allowed to talk to a woman when they are alone, not allowed to touch a woman, not really allowed to even see face to face. When a woman comes to ask something they have to keep their eyes down. They have to look at the tip of their nose so they don't see the woman even by mistake. Because who knows, something might click . . . and one is almost helpless in the hands of love.

They don't stay in people's homes and they don't stay long in one place because attachment, love, becomes possible. So they go on moving, wandering, and avoiding—avoiding all relationships. They have attained a certain quality of stillness. They are undisturbed people, undistracted by the world, but not happy, not celebrating.

In the West just the opposite has happened. People have tried to find happiness through love, and they have created much trouble. They have lost all contact with themselves. They have moved so far away from themselves that they don't know how to come back. They don't know where the path is, where their home is. So they feel meaningless, homeless, and they go on making more and more love efforts with this woman, with that man—heterosexual, homosexual, autosexual. They go on trying every way and again they feel empty, because love alone can give you happiness but there will not be any silence in it. And when there is happiness and no silence, again something is missing.

When you are happy without silence your happiness will be like a fever, excitement . . . much ado about nothing. That feverish state will create much tension in you and nothing will come out of it, just running, chasing. And one day one comes to realize that the whole effort has been baseless because you have been trying to find the other, and you have not yet found yourself.

Both these ways have failed. The East has failed because it tried meditation without love. The West has failed because it tried love without meditation. My whole effort is to give you a synthesis, the whole—which means meditation plus love. One should be able to be happy alone and one should also be able to be happy with people. One should be happy inside and one should also be happy in relationships. One should make a beautiful house inside and outside too. You should have a beautiful garden surrounding your house and a beautiful bedroom too. The garden is not against the bedroom; the bedroom is not against the garden.

> ✿
>
> Meditation should be an inner shelter, an inner shrine. Whenever you feel that the world is too much for you, you can move into your shrine.
> You can have a bath in your inner being.

So meditation should be an inner shelter, an inner shrine. Whenever you feel that the world is too much for you, you can move into your shrine. You can have a bath in your inner being. You can rejuvenate yourself. You can come out resurrected; again alive, fresh, young, renewed . . . to live, to be. But you should also be capable of loving people and facing problems, because a silence that is impotent and cannot face problems is not much of a silence, is not worth much.

Only a silence that can face problems and remain silent is something to be longed for, to be desired.

So these two things I would like to tell you: first start doing meditation, because it is always good to start from the nearest center of your being, and that is meditation. But never get stuck in it. Meditation should move, flower, unfold and become love.

And don't be worried, don't make it a problem—it is not. It is simply human; it's natural. Everybody is afraid—has to be. Life is such that one has to be. And people who become fearless, become fearless not by becoming brave—because a brave man has only repressed his fear; he's not really fearless. A man becomes fearless by accepting his fears. It is not a question of bravery. It is simply seeing into the facts of life and realizing that these fears are natural. One accepts them!

The problem arises because you want to reject them. You have been taught very egotistical ideals: "Be brave." What nonsense! Foolish! How can an intelligent man avoid fears? If you are stupid you will not have any fears. Then the bus driver goes on honking and you stand in the middle of the road, unafraid. Or a bull comes charging at you and you

> A man becomes fearless by accepting his fears. It is not a question of bravery. It is simply seeing into the facts of life and realizing that these fears are natural.

stand there, unafraid. But you are stupid! An intelligent man has to jump out of the way.

If you become an addict and start looking everywhere for the snake in the bushes, then there is a problem. If there is nobody on the road and then too you are afraid and start running, there is a problem; otherwise, fear is natural.

So when I say that you will get rid of your fear, I don't mean that there will be no fears in life. You will come to know that ninety percent of your fears are just imagination. Ten percent are real so one has to accept them. I don't make people brave. I make them more responsive, sensitive, alert, and their alertness is enough. They become aware that they can use their fears also as stepping stones. So don't be worried, mm?

## Why am I still so scared of exposing myself?

Who is not? To expose oneself creates great fear. It is natural, because to expose oneself means to expose all the rubbish that you carry in your mind, the garbage that has been piling up for centuries, for many, many lives. To expose oneself means to expose all one's weaknesses, limitations, faults. To expose oneself ultimately means to expose one's vulnerability. Death . . . To expose oneself means to expose one's emptiness.

Behind all this garbage of the mind and the noise of the mind there is a dimension of utter emptiness. One is hollow without God, one is just emptiness and nothing without God. One wants to hide this nakedness, this emptiness, this ugliness. One covers it with beautiful flowers, one decorates those covers. One at least pretends that one is something, somebody. And this is not something that is personal to you; this is universal, this is the case with everybody.

Nobody can open himself like a book. Fear grips you: "What will people think about me?" From your very childhood you have been taught to wear masks, beautiful masks. There is no need to have a beautiful face, just a beautiful mask will do; and the mask is cheap. To transform your face is arduous. To paint your face is very simple.

Now suddenly to expose your real face gives you a shivering in the deepest core of your being. A trembling arises: Will people like it? Will people accept you? Will people still love you, respect you? Who knows?—because they have loved your mask, they have respected your character, they have glorified your garments. Now the fear arises: "If I suddenly become naked, are they still going to love me, respect me, appreciate me, or will they all escape away from me? They may turn their backs, I may be left alone."

Hence people go on pretending. Out of fear is the pretension, out of fear arises all pseudoness. One needs to be fearless to be authentic.

One of the fundamental laws of life is this: whatsoever you hide goes on growing, and whatsoever you expose, if it is wrong it disappears, evaporates in the sun, and if it is right it is nourished. Just the opposite happens when you hide something. The right starts dying because it is not nourished; it needs the wind and the rain and the sun. It needs the whole of nature available to it. It can grow only with truth, it feeds on truth. Stop giving it its nourishment and it starts getting thinner and thinner. And people are starving their reality and fattening their unreality.

Your unreal faces feed upon lies, so you have to go on inventing more and more lies. To support one lie you will have to lie one hundred times more, because a lie can be supported only by bigger lies. So when you hide behind facades the real starts dying and the unreal thrives, becomes fatter and fatter. If you expose yourself the unreal will die, is bound to die, because the unreal cannot remain in the open. It can remain only in secrecy, it can remain only in darkness, it can only remain in the tunnels of your unconscious. If you bring it to consciousness it starts evaporating.

That's the whole secret of the success of psychoanalysis. It is a simple secret, but the *whole* secret of psychoanalysis. The psychoanalyst helps to bring up all that is inside your unconscious, in the darker realms of your being, to the level of the conscious. He brings it to the surface where you can see it, others can see it, and a miracle happens: even your seeing it is the beginning of its death. And if you can relate it to somebody else—that's what you do in psycho-analysis, you expose yourself to your psychoanalyst—even exposing to a single person is enough to bring great changes in your being. But to expose to a psychoanalyst is limited: you have exposed only to one person, in deep privacy, with the condition that he is not going to make it public. That is part of the profession of the physician, psychoanalyst, therapist; that is part of his oath that he will not tell it to anybody, it will be kept se-cret. So it is a very limited exposure, but still it helps. And it is a profes-sional exposure; still it helps. It takes years, that's why; that which can be done within days takes years in psychoanalysis—four years, five years, and even then psychoanalysis is never complete. The world has not yet known a single case of total psychoanalysis, of the process completed, terminated, finished—no, not yet. Not even your psychoanalysts are completely psychoanalyzed, because the ex-posure itself is very limited and with conditions. The psychoanalyst

> If you expose yourself the unreal will die, is bound to die, because the unreal cannot remain in the open. It can remain only in secrecy, it can remain only in darkness.

listens to you as if he is not listening, because he is not to tell it to anybody. But even then it helps, it helps tremendously to unburden.

If you can expose yourself religiously—not in privacy, not to the professional, but simply in all your relationships—that's what sannyas is all about. It is self-psychoanalysis. It is twenty-four-hour psychoanalysis, day in, day out. It is psychoanalysis in all kinds of situations: with the wife, with the friend, with the relative, with the enemy, with the stranger, with the boss, with the servant. For twenty-four hours you are relating.

If you go on exposing yourself, in the beginning it is going to be really very scary, but soon you will start gaining strength because once the truth is exposed it becomes stronger and the untruth dies. And with the truth becoming stronger you become rooted, you become centered. You start becoming an individual; the personality disappears and individuality appears.

Personality is bogus, individuality is substantial. Personality is just a facade, individuality is your truth. Personality is imposed from the outside; it is a persona, a mask. Individuality is your reality—it is as God has made you. Personality is social sophistication, social polishing. Individuality is raw, wild, strong, with tremendous power.

But the fear is natural because from the very childhood you have been taught falsities, and you have become so much identified with the false that to drop it almost looks like committing suicide. And the fear arises because a great identity crisis arises.

For fifty years, sixty years, you have been a certain kind of person. Now the questioner must be reaching sixty—for sixty years you have been a certain kind of person. Now, at this last phase of your life, dropping that identity and starting to learn about yourself from ABC is frightening. Death is coming closer and closer every day—is this the time to start a new lesson? Who knows if you will be able to complete it or not? Who knows?

> ⤳
>
> Personality is bogus, individuality is substantial.
>
> Personality is just a facade, individuality is your truth.
>
> Personality is imposed from the outside, it is a persona, a mask.
>
> Individuality is your reality—it is as God has made you.

You may lose your old identity and you may not have time enough, energy enough, courage enough to attain to a new identity. So are you going to die without an identity? Are you going to live in the last phase of your life without an identity? That will be a kind of madness, to live without an identity; the heart sinks, the heart shrinks. One thinks, "Now it is okay to go on for a few days more. It is better to live with the old, the familiar, the secure, the convenient." You have become skillful about it. And it has been a great investment, you have put sixty years of your life into it. Somehow you have managed, somehow you have created an idea of who you are, and now I tell you to drop that idea because you are not that!

No idea is needed to know yourself. In fact, all ideas have to be dropped, only then can you know who you are.

Fear is natural. Don't condemn it, and don't feel that it is something wrong. It is just part of this whole social upbringing. We have to accept it and go beyond it; without condemning it we have to go beyond it.

Expose, slowly, slowly—there is no need to take jumps that you cannot manage; go by steps, gradually. But soon you will learn the taste of the truth, and you will be surprised that all those sixty years have been a sheer wastage. Your old identity will be lost, you will have a totally new conception. It will not really be an identity but a new vision, a new way of seeing things, a new perspective. You will not be able to say "I" again with something behind it; you will use the word because it is useful, but you will know all the time that the word carries no meaning, no substance, no existential substance at all; that behind this "I" is hidden an ocean, infinite, vast, divine.

You will never attain to another identity; your old identity will be gone, and for the first time you will start feeling yourself as a wave in the ocean of God. That is not an identity because you are not in it. You have disappeared, God has overwhelmed you.

If you can risk the false, the truth can be yours. And it is worth it, because you risk only the false and you gain the truth. You risk nothing and you gain all.

*I have discovered that I am just bored with myself and I feel no juice. You have said to accept ourselves, whatever we are. I am not able to accept life, knowing that I am missing something of joy inside. What to do?*

I have heard there is a new type of tranquilizer that doesn't relax you—just makes you dig being tense.

Try it! Try it and try it and try it again—be an American!—but not more than three times. Try it, try it, and try it again, and then stop because there is no point in being silly.

You ask me:

"I have discovered that I am just bored with myself . . ."

This is a great discovery. Yes, I mean it! Very few people are aware that they are bored—and they *are* bored, utterly bored. Everybody else knows it except themselves. To know that one is bored is a great beginning; now a few implications have to be understood.

Man is the only animal who feels boredom; it is a great prerogative, it is part of the dignity of human beings. Have you seen any buffalo bored, any donkey bored? They are not bored. Boredom simply means that the way you are living is wrong; hence it can become a great event, the understanding that "I am bored and something has to be done, some transformation is needed." So don't think that it is bad that you are feeling bored—it is a good sign, a good beginning, a very auspicious beginning. But don't stop there.

Why does one feel bored? One feels bored because one has been living in dead patterns given to you by others. Renounce those patterns, come out of those patterns! Start living on your own.

It is not a question of money, power, and prestige; it is a question of what intrinsically you want to do. Do it, irrespective of the results, and your boredom will disappear. You must be following others' ideas, you must be doing things in a "right" way, you must be doing things as they should be done. These are the foundation stones of boredom.

The whole of humanity is bored because the person who would have been a mystic is a mathematician, the person who would have been a mathematician is a politician, the person who would have been a poet is a businessman. Everybody is somewhere else; nobody is where he should be. One has to risk. Boredom can disappear in a single moment if you are ready to risk.

You ask me: "I have discovered that I am just bored with myself . . ." You are bored with yourself because you have not been sincere with yourself, you have not been honest with yourself, you have not been respectful to your own being.

And you say: "I feel no juice." How to feel juice? Juice flows only when you are doing the thing that you wanted to do, whatsoever it is.

Vincent Van Gogh was immensely happy just painting. Not a single painting was sold, nobody ever appreciated him, and he was hungry, he was dying. His brother was giving him only a small amount of money so that he could at least manage to survive—four days a week he would fast, and three days a week he would eat. He had to fast for those four days because otherwise, from where was he going to get his canvases and paints and brushes? But he was immensely happy—his juices were flowing.

> Boredom simply means that the way you are living is wrong, hence it can become a great event, the understanding that "I am bored and something has to be done, some transformation is needed."

He died when he was only thirty-three; he committed suicide. But his suicide is far better than your so-called life, because he committed suicide only when he had painted the thing that he wanted to paint. The day he finished a painting of the sunset, which had been his longest desire, he wrote a letter saying, "My work is done, I am fulfilled. I am leaving this world immensely contented." He committed suicide, but I will not call it suicide. He lived totally, he burned life's candle from both ends together in tremendous intensity.

> It is not a question of money, power, and prestige; it is a question of what intrinsically you want to do. Do it, irrespective of the results, and your boredom will disappear.

You may live a hundred years but your life will be just a dry bone, a weight, dead weight. You say, "You have said to accept ourselves, whatever we are. I am not able to accept life, knowing that I am missing something of joy inside."

When I say accept yourself, I am not saying accept your pattern of life—don't try to misunderstand me. When I say accept yourself, I am saying reject everything else—accept *yourself*. But you must have interpreted it in your own way. That's how things go. . . .

The Martian landed his saucer in Manhattan and, immediately upon emerging, was approached by a panhandler. "Mister," said the man, "can I have a dime?"

The Martian asked, "What's a dime?"

The panhandler thought a minute, then said, "You're right. Can I have a quarter?"

I have not said what you have understood. Reject all that has been imposed upon you—I am not saying accept it. Accept your innermost core that you have brought from the beyond and then you will not feel that you are missing something. The moment you accept yourself without any conditions, suddenly an outburst of joy happens. Your juices start flowing, life really becomes ecstatic.

A certain young man's friends thought he was dead, but he was only in a state of coma. When just in time to avoid being buried he showed signs of life, he was asked how it felt to be dead.

"Dead!" he exclaimed. "I wasn't dead. I knew all the time what was goin' on. And I knew I wasn't dead, too, because my feet were cold and I was hungry."

"But how did that fact make you think you were still alive?" asked one of the curious.

"Well, I knew that if I was in heaven I wouldn't be hungry, and if I was in the other place my feet wouldn't be cold."

One can be certain that you are still not dead: you are hungry, your feet are cold. Just get up and do a little jogging!

A poor man, lacking education and all social graces, fell in love with the daughter of a millionaire. She invited him home to meet her parents at their elegant mansion. The man was intimidated by the rich furnishings, the servants, and all the other signs of wealth, but somehow he managed to appear relaxed—until it came to dinnertime. Seated at the massive dinner table, mellow with the effects of wine, he farted loudly.

The girl's father looked up and stared at his dog that was lying at the poor man's feet. "Rover!" he said in a menacing tone.

The poor man was relieved that the blame had been put on the dog, and so a few minutes later he farted again.

His host looked at the dog and again said, "Rover!" in a louder voice.

A few minutes later he farted a third time. The rich man's face wrinkled in rage. He bellowed, "Rover, get the hell out of here before he shits all over you!"

There is still time—get out of the imprisonment in which you have lived up to now! It only needs a little courage, just a little courage of the gambler. And there is nothing to lose, remember. You can lose only your chains—you can lose your boredom, you can lose this constant feeling inside you that something is missing. What else is there to lose? Get out of the rut and accept your own being—against Moses, Jesus, Buddha, Mahavira, Krishna, accept yourself. Your responsibility is not toward Buddha or Zarathustra or Kabir or Nanak; your responsibility is only toward yourself.

Be responsible—and when I use the word *responsible,* please remember not to misinterpret it. I am not talking about duties, responsibilities, I am simply using the word in the literal sense: respond to reality, be responsible.

You must have lived an irresponsible life, fulfilling all kinds of responsibilities which others are expecting you to fulfill. What is there to lose? You are bored—this is a good situation. You are missing the juice, what more do you need to get out of the prison? Jump out of it, don't look back!

They say: Think twice before you jump. I say: Jump first and then think as much as you want!

## MEDITATION FOR FEAR OF EMPTINESS

Make it a point every night before you go to sleep to close your eyes and for twenty minutes go into your emptiness. Accept it, let it be there. Fear arises—let that be there too. Tremble with fear but don't reject this space that is being born there. Within two or three weeks you will be able to feel its beauty, you will be able to feel its benediction. Once you have touched that benediction, fear will disappear on its own accord. You are not to fight with it.

> ✍
>
> Be responsible—and when I use the word *responsible*, please remember not to misinterpret it. I am not talking about duties, responsibilities, I am simply using the word in the literal sense: respond to reality, be responsible.

Sit kneeling on the floor, or in a comfortable position for you. If your head starts bending forward—it will—allow it. You will almost go into a womb posture, just as the child remains in the mother's womb. Your head will start touching your knees, or touching the floor—just allow it. Enter into your own womb and just be there. No technique, no mantra, no effort—just be there. Just be acquainted with what it is. It is something that you have never known. Your mind is apprehensive because it is coming from a very different and unknown dimension. The mind cannot cope with it. It has never known anything like that before, so it's simply puzzled; it wants to categorize and label it.

But the known is the mind and the unknown is God. The unknown never becomes part of the known. Once it becomes part of the known, it is no more the unknown God. The unknown remains unknowable. Even when you have known it, it remains unknown. The mystery is never solved. The mystery is intrinsically unsolvable.

So every night go into that space. Fear will be there, trembling will be there; that too is okay. By and by the fear will be less and less and rejoicing will come more and more. Within three weeks one day suddenly you will see such blessings arising, such an upsurge of energy, such a joyous quality to your being, as if the night is over and the sun has come on the horizon.

## MEDITATION FOR DISSOLVING OLD PATTERNS OF FEAR

*I've found that I'm still repeating a pattern that I adopted as a child. Whenever my parents scolded me or said anything about me that I felt was negative, I would just shut off, run away, and console myself with the idea that I could do without people, I could manage alone. Now I'm beginning to see that I react to my friends just the same way.*

It is just an old habit that has become rigid. Try to do the opposite of it. Whenever you feel like closing—open yourself. If you want to go, don't go; if you want not to talk, then talk. If you want to stop the argument, don't stop but jump into it with as much vigor as possible.

Whenever a situation arises that creates fear, there are two alternatives—either you fight or you take flight. A small child ordinarily cannot fight, particularly in traditional countries. In America, a child will fight so much that the parents will take the flight! But in old countries, in tradition-bound countries—or in families where the traditional values are still very strong—a child cannot fight. The only way is to close, to wrap oneself inside oneself as protection. So you have learned the trick of flight.

Now the only possibility is that whenever you feel you are trying to escape, stick there, be stubborn, and give a good fight. Just for one month try the opposite and then we will see. Once you can do the opposite you will understand how to drop both. Both have to be dropped, because only then a man becomes fearless—and because both are wrong. Because one wrong has gone too deep in you, it has to be balanced by the other.

So for one month you be a real warrior—about anything. And you will feel very good, really good, mm? Because whenever one escapes, one feels very bad, inferior. This is a cowardly trick—to close oneself. Become brave, mm? Then we will drop both, because to be brave is also, deep down, to be cowardly. When bravery and cowardice both disappear, then one becomes fearless. You try it!

## MEDITATION FOR TRUST

If you feel it difficult to trust, then you have to go back. You have to dig deep into your memories. You have to go into your past. You have to clean your mind of the past impressions. You must be having a great heap of rubbish from your past; unburden it.

This is the key to do it: if you can go back not just as memory, but as a reliving. Make it a meditation. Every day, in the night, for one hour just go back. Try to find out all that has happened in your childhood. The deeper you can go the better—because we are hiding many things that have happened, but we don't allow them to bubble up into consciousness. Allow them to surface. Going every day, you will feel deeper and deeper. First you will remember somewhere when you were at the age of four or five, and you will not be able to go beyond that. Suddenly, a China Wall will face you. But go—by and by, you will see that you are going deeper: three years, two years. People have reached to the point where they were born from the womb. There have been people who have reached into the memories of the womb, and there are people who have reached beyond that, into the other life when they died.

But if you can reach to the point where you were born, and you can relive that moment, it will be of deep agony, pain. You will almost feel as if you are being born again. You may scream as the child screamed for the first time. You will feel suffocated as the child felt suffocated when for the first time he was out of the womb—because for a few seconds he was not able to breathe. There was great suffocation: then he screamed and the breath came, and his passages became open, his lungs started functioning. You may have to move to that point. From there you come back. Go again, come back, every night. It will take at least three to nine months, and every day you will feel more unburdened, more and more unburdened, and trust will arise simultaneously, by the side. Once the past is clear and you have seen all that has happened, you are free of it. This is the key: if you become aware of anything in your memory, you are freed from it. Awareness liberates, unconsciousness creates a bondage. Then trust will become possible.

## MEDITATION FOR TRANSFORMING FEAR INTO LOVE

You can sit in your chair or you can sit in whatsoever posture you feel to be comfortable. Then fold your hands together in your lap, with the right hand underneath the left hand—the position is important because the right hand is joined with the left brain, and fear always comes from the left brain. The left hand is joined with the right brain, and courage comes from the right side.

The left brain is the seat of reason, and reason is a coward. That's why you will not find a man brave and intellectual together. And whenever you find a brave man you will not find an intellectual. He will be irrational, bound to be so. The right brain is intuitive . . . so this is just symbolic, and not only symbolic: it puts the energy into a certain posture, into a certain relationship.

So the right hand goes underneath the left hand and both the thumbs join each other. Then you relax, close your eyes, and let your lower jaw be relaxed just a little—not that you force it—just relaxed so that you start breathing by the mouth. Don't breathe by the nose, just start breathing by the mouth; it is very relaxing. And when you don't breathe by the nose, the old pattern of the mind does not function anymore. This will be a new thing, and in a new breathing system a new habit can be formed more easily.

Second, when you don't breathe through the nose, it does not stimulate your brain. It simply does not go to the brain: it goes directly to the chest. Otherwise a constant stimulation and massage goes on. That's why breathing changes in our nostrils again and again. Breathing through one nostril massages one side of the brain; through another, the other side of the brain. After each forty minutes they change.

So simply sit in this posture, breathing by the mouth. The nose is dual, the mouth is nondual. There is no change when you breathe through the mouth: if you sit for one hour you will be breathing the same way. There will be no change; you will remain in one state. Breathing through the nose you cannot remain in one state. The state changes automatically, without your knowing it changes.

So this will create a very, very silent, nondual, new state of relaxation, and your energies will start flowing in a new way. Simply sit silently doing nothing for at least forty minutes. If it can be done for one hour that will be a great help. So if possible, start with forty minutes, then by and by reach sixty. Do this every day.

And meanwhile don't miss any opportunity; whatsoever opportunity comes, go into it. Always choose life and always choose doing; never withdraw, never escape. Enjoy any opportunity that comes on your way to do something, to be creative.

## AND THE LAST QUESTION: THE FEAR OF GOD

*Is the idea of a personal God who watches out for us, even as a hypothesis, not useful in any way? Because the very idea of dropping the idea of God makes me immensely afraid.*

Why do you feel afraid of dropping the idea of God? Certainly the idea of God is somehow preventing you from being afraid. So the moment you drop it, you start feeling afraid. It is a kind of psychological protection, that's what it is.

The child is bound to be afraid. In the mother's womb he is not afraid. I have not heard that any child in the mother's womb ever thinks of going to the synagogue or to the church or reading the Bible or the Koran or the Gita, or even bothers about whether there is a God or not. I cannot conceive that a child in the mother's womb will in any way be interested in God, in the devil, in heaven, in hell. For what? He is already in paradise. Things cannot be better than they are.

He is completely protected in a warm, cozy home, floating in chemicals that are nourishing. And you will be surprised—in that nine months the child grows more than he will ever grow in ninety years, proportionately. In nine months he travels such a long journey; from being almost nothing he becomes a being. In nine months he passes through millions of years of evolution, from the very first being up to now. He passes through all the phases.

And life is absolutely secure: no need for any employment, no fear of starvation, hunger; everything is being done by the mother's body. Living nine months in the mother's womb in such absolute security creates a problem that has produced your so-called religions.

As the child comes out of the mother's womb, the first thing that happens to him is fear.

It is obvious. His home is lost, his security is lost. His warmth, his surroundings, all that he knew as his world is completely lost, and he is thrown into a strange world, of which he knows nothing. He has to start breathing on his own.

It takes a few seconds for the child to recognize the fact that he has to breathe now on his own—your mother's breathing is not going to help. Just to bring him to his senses the doctor hangs him upside down and hits him on his bottom, hard. What a beginning! And what a welcome!

And just out of that hit he starts breathing. Have you ever observed that whenever you are afraid, your breathing changes? If you have not watched it before, you can watch it now. Whenever you are afraid, your breathing will change, immediately. And when you are at ease, at home, unafraid of anything, you will find your breathing falling into a harmony, in a deep accord, becoming more and more silent. In deep meditation it happens sometimes that you feel as if your breathing has stopped. It does not stop, but it almost stops.

The beginning for the child is fear of everything. For nine months he was in darkness, and in a modern hospital, where he is going to be born, there will be just glaring tube lights all around. And on his eyes, his retina, which has never seen light before, not even a candlelight, this is too much. This light is a shock to his eyes.

And the doctor does not take even a few seconds—he cuts the connection that is still joining him with the mother, the last hope of security . . . and such a tiny being. And you know it perfectly well, that nobody is more helpless than a human child, no other child in the whole existence.

That's why horses have not invented the hypothesis of God. Elephants have not thought about the idea of God; there is no need. The child of the elephant immediately starts walking and looking around and exploring the world. He is not as helpless as a human child. In fact, on the helplessness of a human child depends so much that you may be surprised: your family, your society, your culture, your religion, your philosophy—everything depends on the helplessness of the human child.

In animals, families don't exist for the simple reason that the child does not need the parents. Man had to decide for a certain system. The father and the mother have to be together to look after the child. It is the outcome of their love affair; this is their doing. Now if the human child is left alone, just like so many animals are, you cannot imagine that he is going to survive: impossible! Where is he going to find food? Whom is he going to ask? What is he going to ask?

> Have you ever observed that whenever you are afraid, your breathing changes?
> If you have not watched it before, you can watch it now. Whenever you are afraid, your breathing will change, immediately.

Perhaps he has come too early? And there are a few biologists who think that the human child is born premature—nine months are not enough—because he comes so helpless. But the human body is such that the mother cannot carry the child for more than nine months, otherwise she will die, and her death will mean the death of the child.

It has been calculated that if the child can live in the mother's womb for at least three years, then perhaps there will be no need for a father and mother and the family, and the society and the culture, and God and the priest. But the child cannot live in the mother's womb for three years. This strange biological situation has affected the whole of human behavior, thinking, the structure of family, society; and this has caused the fear.

The first experience of the child is the fear, and the last experience of the man is also fear.

Birth is also a kind of death, you should remember; just look at it from the child's point of view. He was living in a certain world, which was absolutely satisfactory. He was not in any need at all, he was not greedy for anything more. He was simply enjoying being, enjoying growing—and then suddenly he is thrown out.

To the child, this experience is an experience of death: death of his whole world, of his security, of his cozy home. Scientists say that we have not been able yet to create a home as cozy as the womb. We have been trying—all our homes are just efforts to create that cozy home.

We have even tried to make water beds, to give you the same feeling. We have hot bathtubs; lying down in them you can have a little feeling of the child. Those who know how to take a really hot bath will also put salt into it, because in the mother's womb it is very salty—the exact amount of salt that is in sea water. But how long can you lie down in a bathtub? We have isolation tanks that are nothing but a search for the same womb that you have lost.

Sigmund Freud is not an enlightened man—in fact he is a little bit cuckoo, but sometimes cuckoos also sing beautiful songs. Sometimes he has significant ideas. For example, he thinks this idea of man making love to the woman is nothing but an effort to enter the womb again. There may be something in it. This man is crazy, the idea seems to be far fetched; but even if a man like Sigmund Freud is crazy, he has to be listened to very carefully.

I feel that there is something of truth in it: the search for the womb, for the same passage as he had come out from. . . . He cannot reach that womb, that is true. Then he created all kinds of things; he started making caves, houses, airplanes. You see the interior of the airplane—it will not be a wonder if one day you find that in the airplane people are floating in tubs of hot water, salted. The airplane can give you exactly the same situation, but it is not going to be satisfactory.

> Sigmund Freud is not an enlightened man— in fact he is a little bit cuckoo, but sometimes cuckoos also sing beautiful songs.
> Sometimes he has significant ideas.

The child has not known anything else. We try to make it as cozy: just push a button and the air hostess is there. We make it as comfortable as possible, but we cannot make it as comfortable as it was in the womb. You were not needed even to push a button. Even before you were hungry, you were fed. Even before you needed air, it reached you. You had no responsibility at all.

So the child coming out of the mother's womb, if he feels it at all, must feel it as death. He cannot feel it as birth, that is impossible. That is our idea—the idea of those who are standing outside—we say that this is birth.

And the second time, again one day, after his whole life's effort. . . . He has been able to make something—a little house, a family, a small circle of friends, a little warmth, a little corner somewhere in the world where he can relax and be himself, where he is accepted. Difficult—a whole life's struggle, and suddenly, one day, he finds again he is being thrown out.

The doctor has come again—and this is the man who had hit him! But that time it was to start the breathing; this time, as far as we know. . . . Now we are on this side, we don't know the other side. The other side is left to the imagination; that's why heaven and hell . . . and every kind of imagination has gone wild.

We are on this side and this man is dying. To us he is dying; perhaps he is again being reborn. But that only he knows, and he cannot turn back and tell us, "Don't be worried. I am not dead, I am alive." He could not turn in his mother's womb to have a last glimpse and say good-bye to everybody, neither can he turn back now, open his eyes, and say good-bye to you all, and say, "Don't be worried. I am not dying, I am being reborn."

The Hindu idea of rebirth is nothing but a projection of the ordinary birth. For the womb—if the womb thinks—the child is dead. For the child—if it thinks—it is dying. But he is born; it was not death, it is birth. The Hindus have projected the same idea on death. From this side it looks as if he is dying, but from the other side. . . . But the other side is our imagination; we can make it as we want it.

Every religion makes the other side in a different way because every society and every culture depend on a different geography, a different history. For example: the Tibetan cannot think of the other side as cool—even cool is fearful, cold is impossible. The Tibetan thinks that the dead person is warm, in a new world that always remains warm.

The Indian cannot think that it always remains warm. Even four months' heat in India is too much, but for eternity to remain warm—you will be cooked! They had no idea of air-conditioning, but the way the Hindus describe their paradise, it is almost air-conditioned—always cool air, neither hot nor cold, but cool. It is always spring, Indian spring—all the flowers are in blossom, the winds are full of fragrance, the birds are singing, everything is alive; but not warm, cool air. That they remind us again and again: cool air continues to flow.

This is your mind that is projecting the idea; otherwise, for the Tibetan or for the Indian or for the Mohammedan, it cannot be different. The Mohammedan cannot think that the other world is going to be a desert—he has suffered so much in the Arabian desert. The other world is an oasis, an oasis all over. It is not that after a hundred miles you find a small oasis with a little water and a few trees, no—just oases all over, and desert nowhere.

We project, but to the person who is dying it is again the same process that he has experienced once. It is a well-known fact that at the time of death, if the person has not become unconscious, has not fallen into a coma, he starts remembering his whole life cycle. He goes on back to the first moment of his life when he was born. It seems to be significant that when he is leaving this world he may have a look at all that has happened. Just in a few seconds the whole calendar moves, just as it moves in your movies.

That calendar goes on moving, because in a two-hour movie they have to cover many years . . . if the calendar moves at the usual pace, you will be sitting in the movie hall for two years; who is going to be able to afford that? No, the calendar just goes on moving, the dates go on changing, fast. It goes even faster at the time of death. In a single moment, the whole life flashes by and stops at the first moment. It is the same process that is happening again—life has come around full circle.

Why did I want you to remember this? Because your God is nothing but your first day's fear, which goes on and on until the last moment, becoming bigger and bigger. That's why when a person is young he may be an atheist, he can afford to be, but as he grows older to be an atheist becomes a little difficult. If, when he is just coming close to his grave, one foot in the grave, you ask him, "Are you still an atheist?" he will say, "I am having second thoughts"—because of fear: what is going to happen? His whole world is disappearing.

You tell me, "The moment I think of dropping the idea of God, fear comes up." It is a simple indication that with the rock of the idea of God, you are repressing fear; so the moment you remove the rock, the fear springs up.

If the fear comes up, that means you have to face it; it is in no way going to help you to cover it by the idea of God. You cannot have faith again, that is destroyed. You cannot have faith in God, because doubt is a reality, and faith is fiction. And no fiction can stand before a fact. Now, God is going to remain a hypothesis to you; your prayer will be useless. You will know it is a hypothesis, you cannot forget that it is a hypothesis.

Once you have heard a truth it is impossible to forget it. That is one of the qualities of truth, that you don't need to remember it. The lie has to be remembered continually; you may forget. The person habituated to lies needs a better memory than the person who is habituated to truth, because a true person has no need of memory. If you say only the truth there is no need to remember. But if you are saying a lie, then you have to continually remember because you have said one lie to one person, another lie to another person, something else to somebody else. To whom you have said what you have to categorize in your mind and keep. And whenever a question arises about a lie you have to lie again, so it is a series. The lie does not believe in birth control.

Truth is celibate, it has no children at all; it is unmarried in fact.

Once you have understood that God is nothing but a hypothesis created by the priests, the politicians, the power elite, the pedagogues—all those who want to keep you in psychological slavery, who have some vested interest in your slavery. . . . They all want to keep you afraid, always afraid, trembling deep inside, because if you are not afraid, you are dangerous.

> Once you have heard a truth it is impossible to forget it. That is one of the qualities of truth, that you don't need to remember it.

You can either be a person who is a coward, afraid, ready to submit, surrender, a person who has himself no dignity, no respect for his own being—or you can be fearless. But then you are going to be a rebel, you cannot avoid that. Either you can be a man of faith or you are going to be a rebellious spirit. So those people who don't want you to be rebels—because your being rebellious goes against their interests—go on enforcing, conditioning your mind with Christianity, with Judaism, with Mohammedanism, with Hinduism, and they keep you trembling deep inside. That is their power, so anybody who is interested in power, whose whole life is nothing but a will to power, has tremendous use for the hypothesis of God.

If you are afraid of God—and if you believe in God you have to be afraid—you have to follow his orders and commandments, his holy book, his messiah, his incarnation. You have to follow him and his agents.

In fact he does not exist; only the agent exists. This is a very strange business. Religion is the strangest business of all. There is no boss, but there are mediators: the priest, the bishop, the cardinal, the pope, the messiah, the whole hierarchy—and on top there is nobody.

But Jesus derives his authority and power from God—his only begotten son. The pope derives his authority from Jesus—his only true representative, infallible. And it goes on and on to the lowest priest . . . but there is no God; it is your fear. You asked for God to be invented because you could not live alone. You were incapable of facing life, its beauties, its joys, its sufferings, its anguishes. You were not ready to experience them on your own without anybody protecting you, without somebody being an umbrella to you. You asked for God out of fear. And certainly there are con men everywhere. You ask and they will do it for you.

You will have to drop this idea of God that helps you to remain unafraid. You will have to pass through fear and accept it as a human reality. There is no need to escape from it. What is needed is to go deep into it, and the deeper you go into your fear the less you will find it is.

When you have touched the rock bottom of fear you will simply laugh, there is nothing to fear.

And when fear disappears there is innocence, and that innocence is the summum bonum, the very essence of a religious man.

That innocence is power.

That innocence is the only miracle there is.

Out of innocence anything can happen, but you will not be a Christian out of that, and you will not be a Mohammedan out of that. Out of innocence you will become simply an ordinary human being, totally accepting your ordinariness and living it joyously, thankful to the whole existence—not to God, because that is an idea given by others to you.

But existence is not an idea. It is there all around you, within and without. When you are utterly innocent, a deep thankfulness—I will not call it prayer because in prayer you are asking for something, I will call it a deep thankfulness—a gratitude arises. Not that you are asking for something, but thanking for something that has already been given to you.

> You will have to drop this idea of God that helps you to remain unafraid. You will have to pass through fear and accept it as a human reality. There is no need to escape from it.

So much has been given to you. Do you deserve it? Have you earned it? Existence goes on pouring so much over you that to ask for more is just ugly. That which you have received, you should be grateful for it. And the most beautiful thing is that when you are grateful, more and more existence starts pouring over you. It becomes a circle: the more you get, the more you become grateful; the more you become grateful, the more you get . . . and there is no end to it, it is an infinite process.

But remember: the hypothesis of God is gone; the moment you called it a hypothesis the idea of God has been already dropped. Whether you are afraid or not, you cannot take it back; it is finished.

Now the only way left is to go into your fear.

Silently enter into it, so you can find its depth.

And sometimes it happens that it is not very deep.

A story:

A man walking in the night slipped from a rock. Afraid that he would fall down thousands of feet, because he knew that place was a very deep valley, he took hold of a branch that was hanging over the rock. In the night all he could see was a bottomless abyss. He shouted; his own shout was reflected back—there was nobody to hear.

You can imagine that man and his whole night of torture. Every moment there was death, his hands were becoming cold, he was losing his grip . . . and as the sun came out he looked down and he laughed: there was no abyss. Just six inches down there was a rock. He could have rested the whole night, slept well—the rock was big enough—but the whole night was a nightmare.

From my own experience I can say to you: the fear is not more than six inches deep. Now it is up to you whether you want to go on clinging to the branch and turn your life into a nightmare, or whether you would love to leave the branch and stand on your feet.

There is nothing to fear.

# About the Author

Osho is a contemporary mystic whose life and teachings have influenced millions of people of all ages and from all walks of life. He has been described by the *Sunday Times* in London as one of the "1000 Makers of the 20th Century" and by *Sunday Mid-Day* (India) as one of the ten people—along with Gandhi, Nehru, and Buddha—who have changed the destiny of India.

About his own work Osho has said that he is helping to create the conditions for the birth of a new kind of human being. He has often characterized this new human being as "Zorba the Buddha"—capable of enjoying both the earthy pleasures of a Zorba the Greek and the silent serenity of a Gautama the Buddha. Running like a thread through all aspects of Osho's work is a vision that encompasses both the timeless wisdom of the East and the highest potential of Western science and technology.

He is also known for his revolutionary contribution to the science of inner transformation, with an approach to meditation that acknowledges the accelerated pace of contemporary life. His unique "Active Meditations" are designed to first release the accumulated stresses of body and mind, so that it is easier to experience the thought-free and relaxed state of meditation.

# Meditation Resort

~

## Osho Commune International

Osho Commune International, the meditation resort that Osho established in India as an oasis where his teachings could be put into practice, continues to attract thousands of visitors per year from more than one hundred different countries around the world. Located about one hundred miles southeast of Bombay in Pune, India, the facilities cover thirty-two acres in a tree-lined suburb known as Koregaon Park. Although the resort itself does not provide accommodation for guests, there is a plentiful variety of nearby hotels.

The resort meditation programs are based on Osho's vision of a qualitatively new kind of human being who is able both to participate joyously in everyday life and to relax into silence. Most programs take place in modern, air-conditioned facilities and include everything from short to extended meditation courses, creative arts, holistic health treatments, personal growth, and the "Zen" approach to sports and recreation. Programs are offered throughout the year, alongside a full daily schedule of Osho's active meditations.

Outdoor cafes and restaurants within the resort grounds serve both traditional Indian fare and a variety of international dishes, all made with organically grown vegetables from the commune's own farm. The campus has its own private supply of safe, filtered water.

For booking information call (323) 563-6075 in the USA or check osho.com for the Pune Information Center nearest you.

## For more information: www.osho.com

A comprehensive Web site in different languages, featuring an on-line tour of the meditation resort, information about books and tapes, Osho information centers worldwide, and selections from Osho's talks.

Osho International
570 Lexington Avenue
New York, NY 10022
Telephone: (212) 588-9888
Fax: (212) 588-1977
email: osho-int@osho.org.